VON ELIJAH Presents:

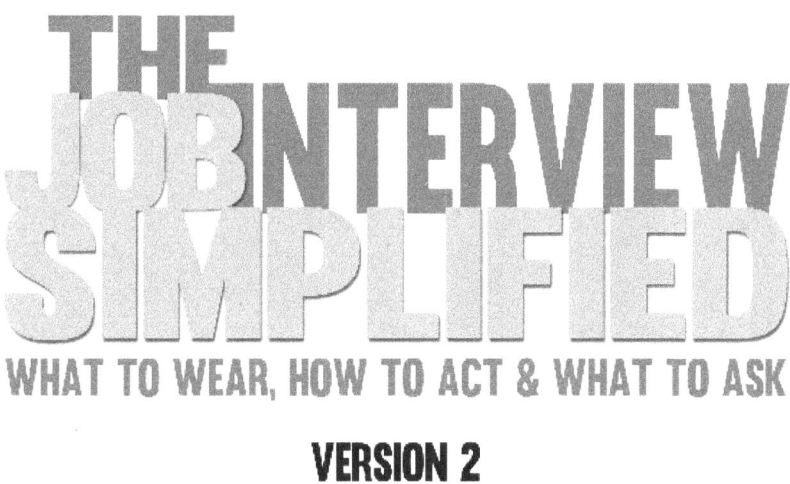

THE JOB INTERVIEW SIMPLIFIED

WHAT TO WEAR, HOW TO ACT & WHAT TO ASK

VERSION 2

Featuring 60 thought-provoking questions to ask your interviewers.

KEEON RUDDER

THE JOB INTERVIEW SIMPLIFIED: 2ND EDITION
by Keeon Rudder

Published by CreateSpace
4900 Lacross Rd
North Charleston, SC 29406
(843) 789-5000

CreateSpace is a registered trademark
of On-Demand Publishing, LLC

Cover design by Jared Williams
and his firm at *DooglesCreativeSolutions.com*

March 2016: Second Edition

While every precaution has been taken in the preparation of this book, the publisher and author assume zero responsibility for errors, omissions, or for damages resulting from the use of the information contained herein.

ISBN-13: 978-1530733194
ISBN-10: 1530733197

To my loving mother, Yvonne Theresa Rudder, who sacrificed her life to ensure my sister and I had the opportunity to succeed

VON

In Loving Memory of

Dan Oren Dinges, Jr., Marcus Deon Henderson,
Mavis Emelia Noel, Stephanie Rena Riley,
and Sandra Debra Fair

Acknowledgments

WRITING BOTH VERSIONS OF THIS BOOK was a wonderful and rewarding journey. This challenge took a few helping hands to document my vast interviewing experiences into an easy to understand format. It is my pleasure to express my appreciation to the people who played a vital role along the way.

First and foremost, my deepest gratitude goes to Sabrina Mendoza. Thank you for advising me so wisely every step of the way. This book would have been vastly inferior if not for your input and feedback.

It took a lot of trust to hand over my unpolished manuscript for feedback, but I was quite pleased with the quality of the critiques I received from my readers. A special thank you to Melissa Wiggins, Shevon Quijano, Joseph and Monica Niles, Jimmy and Claudette Daley, Dee Pipes, Marcus and Melissa Chandler, Ashley Kemp, Brianna McCue, Daniel and Debbie Jackson, Ron and Nellie Biles, Heather Riley, and Terrance Whatley for sharing your invaluable insight, time, and unique perspectives on the manuscript.

To Jared Williams and his firm at *DooglesCreativeSolutions.com* for his hard work in making this manuscript aesthetically appealing. Your graphic design firm has the best staff, display creativity on every project, and was delightful to work alongside.

My editor, Lauren Sweet, for her skillful editorial direction and professionalism.

And finally, a gargantuan thanks to Marcus Whatley for his continual encouragement, patience, sage advice, and life-long friendship. You are a wonderful blessing in my life and I am forever grateful for your kindness towards myself and my family.

Contents

THE JOB INTERVIEW SIMPLIFIED

WHAT TO WEAR, HOW TO ACT & WHAT TO ASK

VERSION 2

It is the obvious which is so difficult to see most of the time.
People say 'It's as plain as the nose on your face.'
But how much of the nose on your face can you see,
unless someone holds a mirror up to you?
—Isaac Asimov

The objective of this book is to give men and women simple, straightforward guidelines to apply for a job, including what to wear to an interview, how to act, and specific questions to ask your interviewer. This book applies to you no matter your background, education, or nationality. Thanks to these guidelines, teenagers will learn how to display respect to impress employers; applicants without college degrees will exhibit competence in order to land their dream job; and college graduates will show perceptive analysis in order to acquire that coveted executive-level position.

This book is unique because its advice is timeless and it educates the reader about the entire interview process. You will be given precise tools to control the flow of conversations, perfect your resume, and you will be taught how best to display confidence during your interview. Most importantly, I provide 60 insightful, open-ended questions for you to ask your interviewers. These questions are not only pertinent to any position for which you may be applying but they will catch the attention of your interviewer, critically engage your interviewer right from the jump, and set the tone for the remainder of the interview. You need to respectfully engage your interviewer in order to learn more about the company, impress your interviewer, and display your intelligence by asking a few of my 60 thought-provoking questions.

This book simplifies the job interview process by breaking it down into ten manageable topics:

- How to Land an Interview
- Preparing for the Interview
- Appearance: What to Wear to Your Interview
- Attitude: How to Display Confidence During Your Interview
- How to Ace a Private Interview
- How to Ace a Public Interview
- Tips for Ex-Convicts
- 60 Specific Questions to Ask Your Interviewers
- Communication Etiquette and Post-Interview Follow-up
- Dealing with Depression

After reading this book, before you walk through the doors for your interview, you will have trained yourself not to think about the rent that is due in ten days, the fact that you have had only twenty dollars to your name for the past two months, or that this is the only company that asked you to come in for an interview.

Instead, you will **be confident that your interviewer will hire you on the spot** because you will have mastered the strategies set forth in this book.

Personal Introduction of the Author

> How you introduce yourself is very important.
> Practice makes perfect.
> —Kendall Hailey

My name is Keeon Rudder, and I am a graduate of The University of Texas at Austin and author of the book *The Purpose of College Simplified: Options after High School, Obtaining Success & Choosing a Career*. Using the techniques in this book, I was hired by employers because I perfected the art of presenting myself as a leader, someone deserving of additional responsibility, a team player, and a man of integrity. I landed my first corporate job in the fast food industry when I was sixteen years old and over the next fifteen years I successfully navigated through multiple interviews in a variety of fields and was hired into both entry-level positions and management roles.

The strategies I have honed will help you land any job in any industry. Throughout the first six years of this process, I switched jobs almost quarterly mostly because of boredom and limited advancement opportunities.

Looking back, I can say with certainty that I felt more challenged and alive, and utilized more of my talents during the interview process than after I was hired. I viewed the interview process as a game in which I used a slew of questions and nonverbal communication to captivate and politely engage my interviewers.

I challenge you to memorize and implement the strategies in this book, tweaking them to fit your personality, so you too will succeed in LANDING ANY JOB IN ANY INDUSTRY!

*Attitude is more important than the past, than education,
than money, than circumstances, than what people do or say.
It is more important than appearance, giftedness, or skill.*
—Charles R. Swindoll

Keynote:

Companies interview people who apply for the position.

Objective:

Utilize multiple platforms to get an invite to interview for a job.

Write Down Your Goals

One of your goals may be to land the job of your dreams but you have no clue where to begin. Well, read this book in its entirety because it will systematically guide you along the often frustrating job search path to help you locate the job of your dreams, land an interview, and ace your interview so that you receive that coveted job offer to join your dream company.

Before you begin to think about which companies you would like to work for, write down all of the goals that you want to achieve. Some goals may directly pertain to your employment search while other goals may implicitly help your chances of landing your dream job by focusing on your Spiritual, intellectual, physical, and social pursuits.

A 1979 Harvard MBA program study depicted the absolute importance of writing down your goals. "In that year, the students were asked, **"Have you set clear, written goals for your future and made plans to accomplish them?"**
Only 3% of the graduates had written goals and plans; 13% had goals, but they were not in writing; and a whopping 84% had no specific goals at all. Ten years later, the members of that class were interviewed again, and the findings, while somewhat predictable, were nonetheless astonishing.
The 13% of the class who had goals were earning, on average, twice as much as the 84% who had no goals at all.
And what about the 3% who had clear, written goals?
They were earning, on average, **ten times as much as the other 97% put together.**"[i]

Writing down your goals matters!! Before you do anything else, **STOP** and **WRITE DOWN YOUR GOALS!**

Strengths and Interests

Next, make another list with three columns and write down your weaknesses, strengths, and interests.

Examples of a few weaknesses:

- Terrible at Math and Science
- Does not delegate well
- Not very good at persuading people to do things
- Afraid to speak in front of others
- Not very good at managing my time without supervision

Examples of a few strengths:

- Excellent at breaking the ice with strangers
- Great organizational skills
- Very good at teaching others to do difficult tasks
- Ability to prioritize tasks mentally
- Inexorable drive till tasks are complete

Examples of a few things that may pique your interests:

- Reading
- Love lending a helping hand to people in need
- Baking
- Love anything related to tennis
- Video games

Keep in mind, your weaknesses can be improved with a little patience and practice. For example, some of you may be terrified to go on job interviews but this book will help you master the interview process.

While you are working to improve your weaknesses, let's focus on your strengths and interests in order to land the job of your dreams.

Clean up ALL of Your Social Media Accounts

Before you take the next step and research industries and companies you would like to work for you need to clean up all of your social media sites. Personally, with the exception of LinkedIn, I strongly recommend that you deactivate—not delete—all of your social media accounts (e.g. Facebook, Twitter, Instagram, Pinterests, etc.). Deleting your accounts will not allow you to recover previous posts, pictures, or any of your social media content, but deactivation will only temporarily remove your social media content which can be reactivated upon your command. During the decision making process, employers will scour the internet to learn as much as they can about you to determine if you are deserving of an interview with their company. After you have signed the employment contract for your new job continue to closely monitor your social media sites.

Should you choose to keep your social media profiles active, be sure to post your job search needs regularly because people cannot help you if they are unaware of your dreams and goals. Equally as important, tag specific individuals within your posts who you believe can help you accomplish your goals because people have the tendency to ignore general posts mistakenly thinking that someone else will help you. Tagging specific people in your employment posts may compel them to lend a helping hand. Make sure to be polite yet specific when asking for help and always thank them for their help afterwards.

While you are cleaning up your social media profiles make certain to do the following:

- Change your settings to private and double check weekly to make sure that interviewers cannot view your posts, pictures, likes, tweets, or comments
- Update your professional profiles on a regular basis
- On social media follow both recruiters and the companies you want to work for and engage them in conversations
- Do not post, like, comment, or retweet anything that could be deemed offensive, illegal, sexually explicit, or profane
- Do not bash your current or former employers
- Be positive and avoid negativity

Huge No-No

We have all heard this response, "I am willing to do anything or work anywhere—I just need a job, any job!"

Never tell someone you are looking for any job because your scope is far too vague and that person might reach out to one maybe two connections in their circle, but that is most likely where their search will end. The job seeker gave them zero helpful information so the helper's brain would almost shut down because they would not know where to even start looking.

Conversely, if job seekers did some leg work on their own to narrow their list to 3–5 companies or industries that interest them, they would likely increase the number of people they are able to recruit to help them achieve their goal.

Choose Your Dream Job

For anyone who already knows what companies and job positions pique your interests—congratulations! However, if you are unsure which companies you would like to work for, let alone which industries intrigue you, do not worry. Your written list of strengths and interests will help you narrow down the extensive list of potential employers to select a handful of companies you would like to join. In the beginning stages of seeking a job, first create a list of industries that interest you.

Examples of a few broad industries:

- Oil and gas
- Medical
- Sales
- Military
- Music/Recording
- Education
- Acting
- Law enforcement
- Entrepreneurship

After you select one or two industries that interest you, Google, research, and choose 3–5 companies within each industry sector that you think you might enjoy working at for a few years. Next, use your list of interests and talents to find positions within each company that best suits your strengths, values, and goals.

Post Your Employment Needs on LinkedIn

If you do not have a LinkedIn profile, take the time to create a free profile today. LinkedIn is a professional, social platform that connects employers, recruiters, employees, and job seekers. It is not necessary to purchase the premium LinkedIn package but if you can afford it there are advantages to being able to send private messages to potential employers or contacts on LinkedIn.

After you have selected three to five companies you would like to work for, post your employment needs regularly on LinkedIn. You may have contacts who can help you but if they are unaware of your needs they cannot assist you. Also, connect with people who currently or previously worked for the companies you like. LinkedIn will tell you if you have mutual acquaintances that work for those companies. If you are lucky enough to have friends who are currently or have been employed at your companies of interest, be sure to message them to inquire if the company is hiring for the position you seek.

If you do not know anyone who works at the company you are seeking to interview with, respectfully introduce yourself to employees currently working for, or previously worked for the business, and politely ask someone at the company who can tell you more about its available positions.

An example of a professional introduction message to a stranger:

Good afternoon, Mrs. Smith,

I hope this message finds you well. We have not had the pleasure of meeting to my knowledge but your help would be greatly appreciated. Would you be so kind as to point me in the right direction please?

My goal is to land full-time employment at your firm as a senior associate.

Would you be willing to introduce me to someone at your firm who can help me accomplish my goal please?

I appreciate any help you are willing to give me. Thank you very much for your time and consideration.

Humbly thankful,
Greg Cooks

Consult with Recruiters / Headhunters

Recruiters and headhunters are also excellent resources to help you acquire employment. There are quite a few benefits to using a recruiter or headhunter:[ii]

- Recruiters are *FREE* and they only get paid when you get hired
- Your recruiter will do most of the leg work for you including the tedious task of sending your resume to potential employers
- Headhunters typically have access to hidden or unpublished internships that have not yet been made public
- Your recruiter can improve your interview skills

✓ Your recruiter will have numerous contacts within the field you are considering

Ask Friends and Family for Referrals

Reach out to friends and family for introductions to contacts— current or former employees—at the firms you selected. Be candid in telling your family and friends that your goal is to work for one of your chosen companies and then ask them for help. Their assistance may come in the form of an introduction to someone who is either currently or has formerly been employed by any of those companies. When your family member or friend gives you the contact information of someone who may be able to help you or they personally introduce you to someone who can point you in the right direction, you must **quickly** and graciously reach out to introduce yourself to the new contact.

An example of sending a professional introduction email to both parties simultaneously in the same email:

Mr. André Smith,

I hope your weekend was fantastic, yet restful. I am touching base because a long-time friend of mine, Danielle Lanza, is seeking full-time employment in the marketing field. She is most astute, interned in the marketing field prior to graduating college, and she is a recent alumnus of the University of Houston——Go Coogs!

André you are well connected and your help would very much be appreciated.

Thank you so much for your continued assistance.

Danielle Lanza,

I would like to introduce you to André Smith, who has an extensive network in the Houston area including a few friends within the Houston marketing industry. I have known André since our stint at The University of Texas at Austin and he has proven himself most resourceful in helping folks I send to him find employment in their respective fields. André is an intelligent, Christian man who daily exhibits the notion of helping those in need and has graciously offered to try to help you. I hope you find his help useful.

André and Danielle, feel free to connect with each other from this moment.

Best wishes,
Kathy McCue

An example of answering a professional introduction email by addressing both parties simultaneously in the same email:

Good morning, Mr. André Smith,

I hope this email finds you well. I was referred to you by Kathy McCue, a good friend of mine, and I am hoping you can point me in the right direction. My goal is to land full-time employment at your firm as a project manager. I had the pleasure of perusing your company website and your firm's accomplishments to date have been nothing short of impressive. In addition, Kathy has had nothing but glowing things to say about you. Would you be so kind as to introduce me to someone at your firm who can help me accomplish my goal?

I am more than happy to email you my resume upon your request. Also, I welcome a phone call to discuss any possibilities you can think of and answer any questions you may have for me.

Kathy McCue,

Thank you for taking time out of your hectic schedule to introduce me to Mr. Smith. I certainly appreciate you going out of your way to help me overcome this next hurdle in my employment pursuit.

With utmost appreciation,
Danielle Lanza

HELPFUL TIPS:

- ✓ Write down your goals and review them at least twice a month.
- ✓ Cleanup ALL of your social media accounts.
- ✓ Post your employment needs on social media and politely ask for help.

SUMMARY NOTES:

1. Companies interview people who apply for positions. Research broad industries that interest you, select 3-5 companies you would like to work for, and apply for the positions you desire.
2. Make a list of your weaknesses, strengths, and interests.
3. Utilize multiple platforms to get invitations to interview for a job.
4. Create and update your professional profiles on a regular basis.
5. Change your social media settings to private and double check weekly to make sure that interviewers cannot view your posts, pictures, likes, tweets, or comments.
6. Follow both recruiters and the companies you want to work for and engage them in conversations through social media.
7. Do not post, like, comment, or retweet anything that could be deemed offensive, illegal, sexually explicit, or profane.
8. Be positive and avoid negativity on social media.

9. Consult with *FREE* Recruiters / Headhunters.

10. Ask friends and family for referrals.

11. Send and respond to introductory emails quickly.

Chapter 2

Preparing for the Interview

> If you fail to plan, then you plan to fail.
> —Harvey MacKay

Keynote:

Companies hire people who are knowledgeable about that company.

Objective:

Tailor your resume to the position for which you are applying.

Read This Book

Preparation for your interview is crucial. Read this book from beginning to end before you begin the interview process, so you will grasp how best to display confidence, master the art of controlling the flow of a conversation, and learn thought-provoking questions to ask your interviewer.

Resume Reviews

More often than not, your resume is the deciding factor in determining if you will be given an opportunity to interview for a position with the firm. Your resume, therefore, must be truthful, mistake-free, and easy to understand.

- Do not lie on your resume, because when your lie is discovered you will instantly lose all credibility
- Keep your resume simple. Do not use fancy fonts, extravagant layouts, or colored paper; these will only serve as an undesirable distraction to your interviewer
- Your resume should ideally not exceed one page and should <u>never</u> extend beyond two pages
- Your employment experiences should never date back further than ten years. Recruiters and interviewers are not interested in work accomplishments that are thirty years old
- Recruiters and interviewers prefer to read key points, bullet points, and concise phrases, so refrain from the use of complete sentences on your resume
- Your email address should include your legal name and should never incorporate more than six numbers. Furthermore, both recruiters and interviewers may make assumptions about you after viewing your email address, so avoid wacky, derogatory, and sexual words within your email address

An example of an inappropriate email address:

Touchme_69_friskycat7499-01/10/2010@bozos.com

An example of a professional email address:

ShannonRadermacher@msn.com

Always quantify your employment experiences by stating measurable results.

- How much money have you saved the company?
- How many new clients have you brought to the firm?
- How much have you increased the firm's profitability each year?
- How many people did you mentor?
- What was your dollar amount in sales each quarter?
- How many companies or potential clients did you prospect daily?
- How many telephone calls did you answer daily?
- How many documents did you review, edit, and submit daily?
- How many hours did you volunteer weekly?
- How much money did you raise quarterly, biannually, or annually?
- How many papers did you grade daily?
- How many quotes and orders did you place daily?
- How many new hires did you train?

- How many advertising or marketing campaigns did you spearhead?
- How many people did you manage?
- How many certifications did you garner?
- How many websites did you build per month?
- How many photography sessions did you have weekly?

An example of quantifying your experience with numbers:

Ineffective – Saved company money by cutting costs.

Effective – Implemented new employee scheduling and payroll systems that saved company $2 million in human resources costs over 4 years.

A second example of quantifying your experience with numbers:

Ineffective — Answered telephone at the front desk.

Effective — Managed switchboard with 8 incoming lines, efficiently answered and routed an average of 800 calls per day.

Avoid filling-up your resume with excessive amounts of frivolous "filler" information that is irrelevant to the job, such as hobbies or interests. However, it is a good idea to succinctly list your hobbies and interests (e.g. karate, painting, swimming, national awards, tennis, golf, husbandry, equestrian, kites, bowling, etc.). Sometimes, interviewers may have the same hobbies as you and that connection might help you during the interview process.

For those who have had limited corporate experience, expand on your academic accomplishments, volunteer hours, and the scholastic subjects in which you excelled.

Be sure to create multiple resumes and tailor each one to the specific position for which you are applying. For instance, if you are applying for three different positions—such as marketing, consulting, and sales—you should submit three different resumes even if all three positions are at the same company.

Save the file under YOUR NAME—RESUME—DATE in your computer and use that description as the subject of your email when you send your resume to the company. If it is simply titled *Resume,* you or a company representative could easily misplace it or it could be confused with another candidate's resume. Lastly, find ten people to assess each of your resumes because fresh eyes can spot mistakes that you might have overlooked. Spelling and grammatical errors will get you dismissed from the interview process faster than the speed of light.

The appearance and layout of your resume are of utmost importance. It can be difficult for job seekers to professionally spice up their resumes without applying color. One possible way for your resume to grab the attention of onlookers can be through formatting. Interviewers may take the time to thoroughly read your resume if it is attractive. Research different resume templates and select layouts that are easy to read and beautiful to look at.

An example of a student's resume with limited corporate experience:

MEGAN RADERMACHER
713-403-1984 | MRadermacher@yahoo.com

EDUCATION
Michigan State University, Isaiah Reid Road, MI   **June 2009**
B.S. in Accounting
Minor: Business Administration
Overall GPA: 3.88

RELATED COURSEWORK
Advanced Financial Accounting   Advanced Federal Taxation
Internal Auditing   International Accounting
Fraud Examination   Managerial Accounting

INTERNSHIPS
Colin & Alan Dixon Accounting Practice   **Spring 2005–Spring 2006**
- 10+ hours weekly
- Prepared tax documents for 310 clients
- Managed the firm's accounting ledger

Murlander LLC   **Summer 2007, Summer 2008**
- 25+ hours weekly
- Reviewed documentation for Litigation Support
- Surveyed 85 Estate Planning & Property Tax appraisals
- Answered 450 clients' questions on accounting procedures

COMPUTER PROFICIENCY
- Utilized QuickBooks to input general ledger and create statistical reports
- Created web pages and brochures utilizing Dreamweaver and Publisher
- Built database to store contact and accounting information

ACTIVITIES/COMMUNITY SERVICE
Beta Alpha Psi - National Accounting Honor Society

Easter Seals – Rehabilitation Clinic
- 300+ hours over 4 years helping with non-profit operations
- Spearheaded the City Wide Hold Up Campaign; Raised $140,000 over 4 years

Wrangler Darlins Spirit Organization
- Documented 220 meetings and reported on Devon West Proceedings
- Participated in revising Jeremy Smith Chapter Constitution

An example of a resume tailored to the interviewee's sales experience:

RON BILES II
76375 Gerren Henry Drive Apt #606
Vida, Texas 40484
RonBiles02@gmail.com
(512) 008-2004

PROFESSIONAL EXPERIENCE

Village Crossfit – Houston, Texas

Inside & Outside Sales Manager   July 2011–Present
- Responsible for the creation of sales targets for all employees
- Responsible for generating leads, providing quotes, and generating sales
- Developed financial models including forecasting, margin analysis, and pricing policy
- Developed monthly strategies for the sales team
- Prepared annual sales budget
- Managed 15 subsidiary sales specialists and ensured all deadlines were met
- Oversaw the design and printing of all marketing merchandise
- Coordinated efforts between the sales team, accountants, web team, MoMo, and the marketing team
- Addressed budgeting issues and other financial matters related to sales
- As the manager, supervised all the sales and marketing personnel
- Coordinated with web team to develop website and e-commerce logistics
- Effectively communicated on various levels with advertisers, corporate clients, and media contacts

Millticket Media – Houston, Texas

Inside Sales Account Manager   December 26, 2007–August 29, 2011
- Responsible for the achievement of the sales target set by the company
- Top 5% of sales force
- Sold over $2,200,000 of information technology equipment
- Prospected 50-80 companies daily
- Provided 50+ quotes and placed 30+ orders for clients daily
- Performed market research and evaluated outcomes with the senior marketing staff
- Maintained and updated the market search and sales reports
- Built and maintained relationships with clients and suppliers
- Procured over 800 new buying accounts including Laurie Gardiner Media
- Prepared market surveys and reports on competitors' strategies

- Increased speed of receivables by 20% to prevent interruption of service to clients
- Created marketing strategies that generated a sales increase of 15%
- Designed attractive presentations for promotional campaigns
- Responsible for providing quotes, generating sales, promoting sales, and marketing

AWARDS / ACCOMPLISHMENTS

Extensive leadership, marketing, and sales experience
Earned Top Honors among the sales team
Trained over 90 new hires
Created marketing strategies that generated a sales increase of 15%

EDUCATION

Texas State University   December 2007
Bachelor of Arts in Corporate Communication

SKILLS / CERTIFICATIONS

Exceptional communication skills, both verbally and written
Energetic and organized, with exemplary customer service skills
Excellent at conflict and problem resolution, with superb leadership, teamwork and management skills
7+ years of experience in the field of sales and the capacity to adopt new concepts quickly

Company Information

The interview process is a two-way street in which both the interviewer and the interviewee are attempting to collect as much information as they possibly can in order to make an informed decision. Your interviewer will be assessing you to determine if you are a good fit for their company but you should also be interviewing the company to decide if the company is an acceptable match for your personality, value system, and short-term and long-term goals.

Take the time to research, in detail, both the company and the position you desire. It is vital for you to understand the history of the firm, some of the names and titles of the company's leaders, and the description of the position for which you want to apply. Generally, that information can be ascertained by searching the company's website; however, there are some additional avenues that can provide more in-depth company information.

Employees are excellent resources from which to gain a wealth of knowledge and their opinions will give you the most accurate depiction of the company. After you browse the company's website, call the company, request to speak to the administrative assistant within the department to which you intend to apply, and ask if they would mind answering a preset list of questions that you have compiled or a few of the sample questions provided.

Sample questions to ask employees:

Question # 1:

How long have you worked for the company?

Question # 2:

What is it like working for the company?

Question # 3:

What are three company perks that you enjoy the most?

Question # 4:

What has been the turnover rate since you worked there?

Question # 5:

What is your biggest problem with the company?

Question # 6:

What are some of your coworkers' grievances with the company?

Question # 7:

What are three things you like about the company?

Question # 8:

What changes would you make at the company or in your position/department?

Question # 9:

What aspect of your job irritates you the most?

Question # 10:

How many people have you helped attain jobs at this company?
Why or why not?

Question # 11:

What is your company's mission? In essence, what does your
company do?

A phone call with the administrative assistant gives you the
opportunity to evaluate:

- The company's culture
- Quality of employees
- The various management styles of managers and owners
- The perceived financial standing of the company
- Various grievances permeating throughout the firm
- How well leaders communicate the company's objectives to
  employees

In addition to the gatekeeper's perspective, if at all possible, be
sure to chat with at least three employees who work in the
department in which you seek to gain employment.

Role Play

Most people are hesitant to practice interviewing strategies in front of others because they fear ridicule or they are scared to make a mistake. If you fear speaking in front of people, remember, *perfect practice makes perfect*. The interview process will become much easier for you the more you practice. Soon you will be just as confident as I am each and every time you walk into an interview.

Practice with someone you trust because their constructive criticism, coupled with the strategies in this book, may be the catalyst that lands you the job of your dreams.

Punctuality

ALWAYS arrive to your interview at least fifteen minutes early but never more than forty-five minutes ahead of time. Map out the route the night before and allow enough time to get to your destination in case you encounter bad traffic. You do not ever want to arrive late for your interview. However, in the rare instance that your tardiness is unavoidable due to an emergency or a car accident, be sure to call the office and speak to either the interviewer or their secretary to alert them to the likelihood of your tardiness. If the incident is severe, inform them of your absence and the need to reschedule. Some companies may be unwilling to reschedule but do not take it personally or give up. There are always more opportunities!

HELPFUL TIPS:

- ✓ Review your work history and memorize employment dates. Potential employers quiz interviewees to make sure the information on their resume is truthful and accurate.
- ✓ Your contact information on your resume must be up to date.
- ✓ Read the book *BRAG! The Art of Tooting Your Own Horn Without Blowing It* by Peggy Klaus to learn how to effectively and succinctly introduce yourself to others.

SUMMARY NOTES:

1. Companies hire people who are knowledgeable about their company. Find out as much information as humanly possible about the company to which you are applying.
2. Do not lie on your resume.
3. Do not use fancy fonts and extravagant layouts on your resume.
4. Your resume should ideally not exceed one page and should never extend beyond two pages.
5. Employment history on your resume should never date back further than ten years.
6. Use bullet points on your resume, rather than complete sentences and paragraphs.
7. Email addresses should include your legal name and fewer than six numbers without inappropriate language or references.
8. Quantify your experiences by stating measurable results.

9.   Succinctly list your hobbies and interests on your resume.

10. Create multiple resumes, tailored to each specific position you apply for.

11. Choose resume templates that grab the attention of onlookers, are easy to read, and beautiful to look at.

12. Find ten people to assess each of your resumes.

13. Question the administrative assistant within your intended department and three employees about the company.

12. Practice the strategies in this book with someone you trust.

13. Arrive at least fifteen minutes early to your interview or contact your interviewer in case of unavoidable delay.

14. Perfect practice makes perfect.

Dress for success. Image is very important.
People judge you by the way you look on the outside.
—Brian Tracy

Keynote:

Companies hire people who dress professionally and present themselves with class.

Objective:

Stand out so your interviewer will remember you.

Dress to Impress

The outfit you choose for your interview is important but before you lay out your wardrobe, there are some accessories you should always take to your interview:

- A leather folder that opens up, so you can file papers and store a notepad. Inside the folder should be:
- Ten copies of your most current resume
- Two pens with blue or black ink
- A copy of my list of 60 questions from chapter eight

VE In addition, bring samples of your work including your portfolios, if applicable.

No matter what you choose to wear to your interview make certain that your entire outfit is professional, wrinkle-free, stain-free, hole-free, and well-fitting. The most universally accepted outfit to wear to an interview is a business suit for men and a pants or skirt suit for women. Gentlemen, there are a few restrictions on how you should wear your suit; for example, you can wear it with or without a tie, jacket, or socks. You can even mix and match your suit jackets and pants to further demonstrate your individuality or personality. There are a few faux pas you should not commit. For instance, make sure your belt always matches the color of your shoes, your hair should be neatly styled out of the face and eyes, and facial hair must be trimmed or removed completely.

It is also acceptable for both men and women to wear a "business casual" outfit to your interview but remember there is a very fine line between an ensemble that exemplifies fashionable trends and an outfit that displays blatant disrespect or disorder. If you are ever in doubt, put on a sports coat or opt out of possibly under-dressing, and instead wear a suit. Jeans are permissible options for interview attire, provided they are free of holes, writing, and distress marks, if the corporate culture is very casual; however, if you do wear jeans, I highly recommend you wear a sports coat over your Polo, button down, pull over, or sweater to appear more professional.

When worn properly, business casual attire can be an effective tool to help you stand out, especially when the majority of your fellow interviewees choose to wear a typical business suit. No matter what style you choose, wear clothing that complements your personality, that you are comfortable in, and makes you feel courageous.

Women's outfits should also be wrinkle-free, stain-free, hole-free, and well-fitting. Be sure to avoid cleavage exposure, remember that your heels should never be higher than two inches, and if wearing a skirt rather than slacks, the skirt must be at least knee-length, preferably coupled with a pair of nude or black pantyhose. Your hairstyle, jewelry, and makeup should be modest unless you are interviewing for a job in the fashion industry. If you are ever in doubt, wear a tailored pants suit with a nicely complementing blouse. A good rule of thumb is to look at yourself in the mirror before your interview and if you say to yourself, "I look hot!" go back to your closet and change. Looking "hot" may be acceptable in your free time but is guaranteed to give the wrong impression to your interviewer, almost certainly ensuring your interview will be unsuccessful.

Clothing NEVER to Be Worn

Equally as important, **<u>DO NOT WEAR</u>** tennis shoes, basketball shoes, sandals, athletic wear, any kind of shorts or tee shirts, capris, tight-fitting clothing, or a hat/ball cap to your interview.

Dress shoes, non-decorative cowboy boots, high heels, and boots are usually considered appropriate business attire, while tennis shoes, sandals, and basketball shoes are viewed as lackadaisical, unprofessional, and immediately give the interviewer a negative first impression of the interviewee. Furthermore, if you have tattoos or visible piercings, cover them if possible.

Men should remove all of your earrings, neck jewelry, and any visible jewelry aside from your wedding band or watch. After your interview is over and you leave the building, you are free to wear these items. However, in professional environments they are most often viewed as inappropriate and distracting.

Although it is common for women to have multiple ear piercings, do not wear more than two earrings in each ear to your interview. Studs or short earrings are usually preferred to large, or low dangling earrings, which can be distracting and noisy. Also, be sure to remove any visible piercings including tongue and nose rings because they are unacceptable in a professional environment.

Make sure to wear an outfit that feels comfortable and boosts your confidence because confidence is an essential key to a successful interview.

HELPFUL TIPS:

- ✓ Shoes should be polished and unblemished.
- ✓ ALWAYS turn off your cell phone or put it on silent before you go into your interview. Do not make calls, or answer texts or phone calls during your interview or in the presence of your interviewer.
- ✓ Chewing gum is unprofessional: opt for breath mints instead.
- ✓ Your cologne or perfume should be minimal or nonexistent. Always be aware of the possibility that your interviewer may have allergies or sensitivities to strong scents that would interfere with your interview.

SUMMARY NOTES:

1. Companies hire people who dress professionally and present themselves with class.
2. Bring a leather folder, ten copies of your most current resume, two pens with blue or black ink, and your portfolio to your interview.
3. Your outfit must be wrinkle-free, stain-free, hole-free, and well-fitting.
4. The most universally accepted outfit to wear to an interview is the business suit for men and the pants or skirt suit for women.
5. Your belt must always match the color of your shoes.
6. Do not wear tennis shoes, basketball shoes, sandals, athletic wear, any kind of shorts or tee shirts, capris, tight-fitting clothing, or a hat/ball cap to your interview.

7. Cover up your tattoos, keep make up and perfume/cologne to a minimum, and remove any excessive jewelry including facial piercings or distracting pieces.

8. Men, if you are ever in doubt, put on a sports coat with your business casual outfit.

9. Women should avoid cleavage exposure, heels should never be higher than two inches, and skirts must be knee-length and worn with pantyhose.

10. Ladies, your hairstyle, jewelry, and makeup should be modest.

11. Ladies, if you are ever in doubt, wear a well-fitting pants or skirt suit with a nice blouse.

12. Ladies, if you look in the mirror and say to yourself, "I look hot!" go back to your closet and change.

13. Wear clothing that complements your personality and makes you feel courageous.

A positive attitude causes a chain reaction
of positive thoughts, events and outcomes.
It is a catalyst and it sparks extraordinary results.
—Wade Boggs

Keynote:

Companies hire people who *appear* confident.

Objective:

Practice the following strategies daily until they become second nature to you.

Mental Confidence Builders

Your attitude throughout the entire interview process is the single most important factor that will influence your interviewer. It does not matter whether your knees are shaking, your palms are sweating, or your armpits are drenched. When you use the strategies in this chapter, your interviewer will think you are the most confident person in the world.

The first step to *appearing* confident is to believe that your interviewer will hire you on the spot. Do not pretend; instead believe with all of your heart that you will be offered the position. As a matter of fact, write down specific corporate goals you wish to achieve during your tenure, list potential people working for the company or outside of the company who you would like to mentor you, and jot down positive corporate changes you seek to make. It is imperative you begin to picture yourself working for the company in question because **SUCCESS MUST FIRST BE VISUALIZED BEFORE IT CAN BE ATTAINED**.

The second step to *appearing* confident is to have the mindset that you are the perfect person for the job! You have already completed the most difficult phase of the interview process, which is to receive an interview. So, literally take a deep breath, exhale, and pat yourself on the back. You were called in for an interview because you caught your interviewer's attention and your interviewer already has a hunch that you are the perfect person for the position. Now comes the easy part. Your upcoming interview is simply an opportunity for you to further impress your interviewer. The moment you walk into your interview, you should be confident in knowing that your interviewer is excited about hiring you.

Nonverbal Communication

The third step to *appearing* confident comes before your verbal interview begins—the handshake. Your handshake should be firm without applying too much pressure on the interviewer's hand. Do not squeeze too tightly and hold on to the other person's hand for approximately three seconds. Also, be sure to make eye contact with the recipient of the handshake and do not twist the other person's hand to place your hand at the top or the bottom.

The fourth step to *appearing* confident is to make consistent eye contact with your interviewer. Now, you do not want to stare creepily into their eyes or stare at their lips as though you want to kiss them, but do not gaze aimlessly around the room either. To improve your eye contact proficiency, practice looking directly into someone's eyes for an entire conversation and focus specifically on decreasing the number of times you break eye contact. Be sure to incorporate an occasional head nod to confirm that you comprehend what the other party is saying and project a gentle smile of interest. Consistent eye contact combined with an occasional head nod and a gentle smile shows self-confidence, respect, and interest in what your interviewer is saying.

The fifth step to follow, if you have sweaty palms like me or tend to fidget with your fingers when you speak, is to clasp your hands together and place them in your lap for the duration of the interview. Constant hand movement is not only distracting but it indicates nervousness, while clasped hands resting in your lap depicts self-control, poise, and dignity.

For men, this sixth suggestion may be tough to believe but rest assured it conveys a high level of maturity, sophistication, and class. Cross your legs at the knees for the full interview, though keep in mind you are permitted to switch legs when necessary. This may take some time before it feels comfortable but remember *perfect practice makes perfect.*

Ladies, also remember that no matter how nervous you may be, avoid crossing your legs at the knees. Instead, sit towards the edge of your chair, angle yourself, and cross your legs at the ankles while keeping your knees discreetly together. Nothing is worse than realizing too late that the skirt which was a perfectly acceptable length while standing, is now inappropriately short and revealing after crossing your legs.

Men and women who have a high voice, try lowering the pitch of your voice slightly so as not to appear obnoxiously nervous or simpering. Equally, if your voice is particularly low, try raising the pitch of your voice just a bit to appear friendlier and less abrasive. Also, flirtatious speech and overly casual language (for example, "um", "like", "oh my God", "you know what I mean", "you feel me", etc.) should never be used. Finally, sit upright because aside from being a healthy habit, perfect posture exudes character, grace, and interest in the conversation.

Dining Etiquette

Many interviewers take job candidates out to breakfast, lunch, or dinner to assess their social skills and table manners. The following suggestions will allow you to project both confidence and competence throughout your dining experience. First, visit the restaurant's website or go to the restaurant before your interview to see what items are on the menu, so that you will know exactly what you want to order ahead of time. Second, be polite to your server or waiter, always remembering to cordially say "please" and "thank you". If your server does not state their name during their introduction, be sure to ask for their name. Refrain from using the server's last name; instead, use their first name with each request you make and when you thank them after each completed task.

An example of being polite to your server:

Brandon Lathan, Candidate:

"Amanda, may I get a sweet iced tea with some extra lemons, please?"

Amanda Sheffield, Server:

"Absolutely and is everything all right for you, ma'am?"

Margot Delaronde, Interviewer:

"Everything is perfect. Thank you, Amanda."

You must be able to differentiate between all the dining utensils and know the specific use of each one. The easiest way to remember which utensil to use is to start at the outside and work your way in. Your salad fork will be on the far left of your plate and your entrée fork will be next to it closer to your plate. Your spoons and knives will be to the right of your plate with your knife placed closest to your plate, to the left of your spoons. Remember that your teaspoon is typically smaller than the soupspoon and may also be used to stir coffee. Your dessert spoon and fork will be placed directly above your plate, while your bread plate will be at the top left of your place setting, and any liquids will be at the top right.

Similar to life, there are exceptions to some dining rules. For instance, your butter knife may be found on the right side of your plate or directly on the butter plate; your dessert fork may actually sit to the left of your plate next to your entrée fork; the fish fork, if needed, can be placed on the right side of the plate, and sometimes, a larger steak knife may rest above your plate.

Remember the basics of table etiquette: place your napkin on your lap after everyone is seated, keep your elbows off of the table, sit up straight, do not stab your food, and chew small bites with your mouth closed which will allow you room to speak if needed.

When pausing or after finishing your meal, never place used utensils back on the tabletop, but instead lay them neatly across your plate. If you excuse yourself from the table, place your napkin on your seat or the arm of your chair, but not on the table or over your place setting.

Men, if you are dining with a woman, stand each time she approaches or leaves the table.

Do not drink alcohol before or during your interview. Your interviewer(s) may order alcohol for themselves and they may even ask you if you would like a similar drink, but do not accept. Politely say, "No, thank you." every time.

When you are offered a roll set the roll on your bread plate. If you require butter, take butter from the butter dish with your butter knife and put it on the bread plate—not directly onto the bread. Be sure to break your roll into bite-sized pieces, spread the butter onto each piece as you eat it, and eat only one piece at a time. Also, do not wipe your plate with your roll.

Avoid ordering messy food. For example, saucy pasta, chicken with bones, meatball sandwiches, ribs, hamburgers, tacos, large sandwiches, and whole lobsters have the potential to cause you embarrassment. Also, be considerate and do not order the most expensive or the cheapest entrée on the menu.

Remember that though you may not feel hungry due to nerves, you must order something to eat; nothing makes someone more uncomfortable than a person twenty inches away just staring at them as they eat.

Do not eat your meal too fast or extremely slowly. Do your best to match your interviewer's eating pace and only order dessert if your interviewer does so first. Also, if you are unable to finish your meal, do not ask for a doggie bag or takeout box.

After you have finished eating, rest the utensils that you used on the plate from which you have eaten, rather than putting your dirty utensils on the tablecloth or placemat. Set your utensils at the top of your plate to signal the waiter that you are finished.

Last but not least, remember to say "thank you" to your interviewer at least three nonconsecutive times after the conclusion of the meal.

HELPFUL TIPS:

- ✓ Do not badmouth or speak negatively of your former employer or coworkers during your interview. Keep your speech positive throughout the process.
- ✓ While you wait in the lobby for your interview, practice your *nonverbal communication*.
- ✓ If being interviewed at a restaurant, arrive at the restaurant before your interviewer and wait in the lobby, not at the bar. Always check to see if your party is already there.
- ✓ If something is wrong with your order and the mistake is not life-threatening, let it slide.
- ✓ The proper way to eat soup is to spoon it away from your body so you do not spill it in your lap. NEVER slurp from your spoon.
- ✓ Say "*yes please*" or "*no thank you*" instead of simply saying "*yes*" or "*no*" in response to questions.
- ✓ Allow your interviewer to pay for the tab. The person who extended the invitation will expect to pay both the bill and the tip.

SUMMARY NOTES:

1. Companies hire people who *appear* confident.
2. Your attitude throughout the entire interview process is the single most important factor that will impress your interviewer.
3. Believe that your interviewer will hire you on the spot.
4. Tell yourself that you are the perfect person for the job.

5. Remind yourself that the interviewer already likes you.

6. Make consistent eye contact with your interviewer.

7. Your handshake should be firm but do not hold the other person's hand for more than three seconds.

8. During the interview, clasp your hands together and place them in your lap.

9. Gentlemen, cross your legs at the knees.

10. Ladies, cross your legs at the ankles and sit more towards the edge of your chair.

11. Do not use flirtatious speech or overly casual language.

12. When being interviewed at a restaurant, know exactly what you want to order ahead of time.

13. Be extremely polite to your server or waiter.

14. Learn to differentiate between all the dining utensils and know their uses.

15. Do not drink alcohol before or during your interview.

16. Do not order messy food.

17. Remember to say "thank you" to your interviewer at least three non-consecutive times after the meal.

18. Perfect practice makes perfect.

He explained to me with great insistence that
every question possessed a power that did not lie in the answer.
—Elie Wiesel

Keynote:

Companies hire people who coax their interviewers to talk for an extended amount of time.

Objective:

Master *open-ended* and *follow-up* questioning.

Private Interviews

Ironically, the terms *private* and *public* interviews have nothing to do with the location of the interview, instead they hint at the format and the atmosphere of the interview.

More often than not, private interviews give both the interviewee and the interviewer opportunities to ask each other questions, which allow for more casual discourse between the two parties. Typically, the atmosphere in a private interview tends to be friendlier, jovial, and encompass more personal questions than a public interview.

Most interviewees have a tendency to talk as much as they can, and some even try to answer every question with excessive amounts of detail. Unfortunately, both approaches are severely flawed and can give your interviewer a negative impression of you.

Your main goal in private interviews should be to get your interviewer to talk for at least two-thirds of the interview, via *open-ended* and *follow-up* questioning, while you decide if the company is a good fit for you. People enjoy talking about themselves even more so when the topic at hand pertains to their personal or corporate achievements. When your interviewer is speaking, sit quietly with your legs crossed, respond nonverbally with head nods and gentle smiles, take notes when applicable, make uninterrupted eye contact with your interviewer, and offer clarifications to your inquiries and answers only when prompted to do so by your interviewer.

Open-ended Questions

You have the power to control the flow of the conversation in a private interview simply by asking questions. You can make the other party talk for as long as you desire. Your questions can discreetly change the subject and take a conversation in any direction you choose.

The most basic forms of questioning are *open-ended* and *closed-ended* questions. An open-ended question does not suggest possible answers and is designed to encourage a full, meaningful answer. Conversely, a closed-ended question is a form of question which can normally be answered using a simple "*yes*" or "*no*". You need to become proficient in open-ended questioning and forgo the usage of closed-ended questions.

An example of a closed-ended question:

Ron Henry:

"Did you eat breakfast this morning?"

Kellen Hood:

"No."

An example of an open-ended question:

Ryan Dixon:

"What did you eat for breakfast this morning?"

Lauren Thomas:

"I made banana pancakes drenched in delicious buttermilk syrup, and an omelet filled with lots of seasonings including onions and kale lettuce. Oh, and to top it off I sprinkled some of my aunt's homemade salsa on top of the omelet. It was delightful!"

Follow-up Questions

The second form of questioning that you must skillfully master is the follow-up question. A follow-up question is an immediate, on-the-spot question that addresses a statement or an answer to a previous question. Follow-up questions seek clarification, ask for elaboration, and can be asked every time someone opens their mouth to speak. Follow-up questioning is a useful tool to get the other party to continue to talk.

An example of an open-ended, follow-up question:

Ryan Dixon:

"That's awesome! Your aunt makes homemade salsa. What are some other dishes that she makes from scratch?"

Lauren Thomas:

"She makes almost everything from scratch: pasta sauce, beef-a-roni, stuffing, pork roast, and my favorite, sweet potato casserole."

A second example of an open-ended, follow-up question:

Ryan Dixon:

"It sounds like you have some talent in the kitchen yourself. What are three of your absolute favorite dishes to cook?"

Lauren Thomas:

"I have so many that it's really hard to pick. Let's see. I love cooking enchiladas, brick chicken with couscous, and migas."

In the examples given, Ryan asked two excellent open-ended, follow-up questions to get Lauren to continue to talk and elaborate on her original answer. At this juncture, Ryan could continue his cooking inquiries or he could choose to discreetly change the subject.

Discreetly Changing the Subject

Both open-ended and follow-up questions give you the power to change the subject at will, entice the other person to talk for an extended period of time, and possibly avoid answering certain questions entirely. **<u>Generally, folks feel obligated to answer a question</u>. By answering that inquiry with a different question, it is possible to avoid having to answer the first and therefore, change the subject and control the flow of conversation.**

An example of changing the subject for beginners:

Lorraine Barfield, Interviewer:
"What was your GPA at Stanford University?"

Zac Lampkin, Candidate:
"Thanks to a high GPA my first year at Stanford University, I was accepted into the prestigious Tau Beta Pi Honor Society for engineering students with distinguished GPAs."

Zac did a fantastic job of partially answering the question, without directly giving his interviewer a quantifiable answer.

Notice also that he **did not lie** about his GPA. Furthermore, Zac's partial answer entices his interviewer to ask him about his experience in the Tau Beta Pi Honor Society, which would discreetly change the subject. However, if a perceptive interviewer persisted in asking about his GPA, then Zac would be forced to eventually answer the interviewer's original question numerically.

An example of changing the subject for the advanced:

Richard Harris, Interviewer:

"What was your GPA at Texas A&M University?"

Nicole Vassiliades, Candidate:

"My second year I was accepted into the prestigious Sigma Beta Delta Honor Society for business students with distinguished GPAs. Speaking of which, were you involved in similar organizations when you were in college?"

Richard Harris, Interviewer:

"Well, I was a member of the Tau Sigma Delta Honor Society and the Sigma Lambda Alpha Honor Society for Greek fraternity and Architecture students."

Nicole Vassiliades, Candidate:

"Wow! That is impressive! What fraternity did you join? And what were your favorite classes while you were in school?"

Nicole did an excellent job of:

- ▲ Partially answering the question
- ▲ Conveying humility by utilizing an introductory phrase *("Speaking of which")*
- ▲ Successfully avoiding answering the interviewer's question by asking an open-ended question *("were you involved in similar organizations when you were in college?")*. If Nicole was unsure if the interviewer went to college, she could instead ask *"are you familiar with Sigma Beta Delta Honor Society?"*
- ▲ Discreetly changing the subject by asking two open-ended, follow-up questions *("What fraternity did you join? And what were your favorite classes while you were in school?")*

Once again, Nicole **did not lie** about her GPA, but if a perceptive interviewer utilizing the STAR technique (STAR is covered in *Chapter 6: How to Ace a Public Interview*) were to redirect the conversation back to her GPA, then she would be forced to eventually answer the interviewer's original question numerically.

This method is a wonderful tool but **do not overuse it by avoiding too many of the interviewer's questions** or you run the risk of annoying them. I cannot stress enough the importance of using a humble introductory phrase and speaking as politely as possible.

Your posture, nonverbal communication, and most notably, your tone of voice are extremely important, and they must all work cohesively to portray humility or else you will most assuredly give the wrong impression, thus ensuring a negative end to the interview.

An example of avoiding a question for the advanced:

Janie Munoz, Interviewer:

"What is the most difficult decision you had to make within the last four years and how did you solve it?"

Lloyd Fair, Candidate:

"I'm sorry, but earlier you mentioned that accountability was an important asset for this position. Can you quickly delineate which facets of accountability link more closely to this position?"

Lloyd eloquently avoided the interviewer's questions by reverting the conversation to a former statement of accountability posed by the interviewer.

- He displayed humility by using an introductory phrase *("I'm sorry, but earlier you mentioned")*
- Then he confidently asked the interviewer an open-ended question *("Can you quickly delineate which facets of accountability link more closely to this position?")* that was totally unrelated to the interviewer's most recent questions

This method of questioning takes months of practice and a confident yet humble demeanor to successfully execute. Your tone of voice is of utmost importance because you do not want to appear disrespectful, combative, or demeaning.

Remember to speak confidently but do not yell; instead, smile gently, and portray a calm inquisitive tone that gives the impression you really want to learn. In addition, use some of the following introductory phrases to help convey humility before you try to change the subject or avoid answering a question altogether:

- I'm sorry, but earlier you mentioned
- If I may ask
- Speaking of which
- I am intrigued
- Would you mind clarifying something for me please
- I have a question
- I was thinking
- Come to think of it
- Please correct me if I am wrong
- I really liked your viewpoint
- It just now crossed my mind that what you said earlier makes perfect sense
- It just dawned on me
- Thinking back to what you said earlier
- What you said earlier was spot on
- I absolutely agree with what you stated earlier

\E Oh, now I understand

\E Thank you for clarifying

Do not attempt to implement this line of questioning until you have first mastered *open-ended* and *follow-up* questioning. Practice these two techniques daily because during your private interview you will have to control the flow of conversation whenever possible by asking open-ended and follow-up questions. After you have perfected these strategies, do everything in your power to speak less than your interviewer. However, I strongly suggest you do not avoid too many of the interviewer's questions.

HELPFUL TIPS:

- ✓ The most valuable of all talents is that of never using two words when one will do. —Thomas Jefferson
- ✓ For phone interviews, choose a quiet and secluded place to conduct the interview.
- ✓ If you want to really impress your interviewer, pay very close attention to detail. For example, make sure your name and the current date appear at the top of all paperwork.

SUMMARY NOTES:

1. Companies hire people who *display* excellent conversational skills.
2. Your goal is to get your interviewer to talk more than you do.
3. Master asking *open-ended* questions.
4. Practice asking *follow-up* questions.
5. Perfect your ability to control the flow of conversations by asking questions.
6. Do not overuse the tools to discreetly change the subject.
7. Perfect practice makes perfect.

Nothing can stop the man with the right mental attitude from achieving his goal; nothing on earth can help the man with the wrong mental attitude. —Thomas Jefferson

Keynote:

Companies hire people who are concise and direct when answering questions.

Objective:

Repeat every question out loud then align all answers to the position you seek.

Public Interviews are Challenging

Public interviews have little to do with the location of the interview, instead it hints at the format of an interview. In fact, there are three prevalent differences between public and private interviews.

One major distinction is that public interviewers are generally not permitted to answer any of the interviewee's questions, thus rendering the interviewee's *open-ended* and *closed-ended* questioning useless (For more information, refer back to *Chapter 5: How to Ace a Private Interview*).

In addition, public interviewers are typically not allowed to give clarification to any of their questions and the interviewer cannot move on to their next question unless their current question is answered by the interviewee, thus rendering the interviewee's attempt to *discreetly change the subject* virtually impossible (Refer to *Chapter 5: How to Ace a Private Interview* for further information).

Public interviewers have a preset list of questions they are required to ask every interviewee and they are not permitted to stray from that list. Also, some public interviewers are required to write down or record the answers of every interviewee's answer in order to compare all job candidates' responses.

STAR Questions

Most public interviewers utilize behavior-based interview questions or STAR questioning, which compels interviewees to provide detailed, solid answers to an interviewer's questions.

Public interviewers ask situational questions to learn about recent challenges the interviewee faced, the tasks the interviewee hoped to achieve at the end of the challenge, specific actions taken by the interviewee to rectify the situation, and the final results or outcome which can conclude with lessons the interviewee learned from the experience.

Sample STAR questions interviewers ask

Question # 1:

Describe a situation where you disagreed with a superior.

Question # 2:

Tell me about a time where you had to solve a difficult problem.

Question # 3:

Do you work well under pressure? If so, describe a time where you had to do so.

Question # 4:

Give me one example of a time when you motivated others.

Question # 5:

Tell me about a time where you delegated tasks during a project.

Question # 6:

Tell me about a time when you missed an obvious solution to a problem.

Question # 7:

Tell me about your proudest professional accomplishment.

Question # 8:

Tell me about a time you experienced conflict at work.

How to Answer STAR Questions

STAR questions essentially force the interviewee to give their answers in the form of a story. Public interviewers closely observe the interviewee's thought process, their approach to problem solving, their rationalization of proposed solutions, and their ownership of the situation's outcome. Public interviewers also assess the interviewee's ability to verbalize past experiences that shows the interviewee has already applied the necessary skills required for the position the interviewee is currently applying.

The best way to organize and answer behavioral questions is to use the STAR method—Situation, Task, Action, Result—which provides a simple framework for interviewees to use when they craft their answers. Remember to quantify your experiences in each of your answers (Refer back to *Chapter 2: Preparing for the Interview* if you need a refresher course on quantifying your experiences).

Situation:

This is the beginning of the story where the interviewee paints a clear picture of the who, what, when, where, and the problem that needed to be solved. An interviewee's response should typically begin like this: "Two years ago when I was working for *Authority Solutions* in Houston, Texas as a Search Engine Optimization expert, a prospective client called and wanted to increase her website traffic in three months, which was half the time we normally tell our clients they can expect to begin to see a positive return on their SEO investment."

Task:

The next portion of the interviewee's answer should explain the specific role they played in the situation, the plan of action to address each of the problems, touch on the desired outcome, and how they were able to spin the situation into an opportunity. The interviewee's answer may sound like this: "I took this opportunity to invite her to visit our office for lunch and a quick tour while I patiently listened to her business needs. This visit to our office allowed her to meet our team in person, hear of our many success stories, and to see firsthand that we cared more about helping her achieve her goals than us making a few dollars."

Action:

The next part of the interviewee's answer should discuss the steps taken to solve the challenges, the specific actions taken by the interviewee to overcome roadblocks, and the interviewee's thought process for each step. Make sure to present your story in sequential order and talk about the step-by-step actions you took using lots of detail. This will certainly help the interviewer understand your contributions to the situation.

Result:

The last part of the interviewee's story should summarize the tangible results of their hard work. Focus on lessons learned even when the outcome was negative and be sure to quantify the results. The interviewee's final response may sound like this: "We successfully gained her as a client and increased her website traffic by 20% in five months. Although we made a few mistakes along the way with her account, my immediate supervisor was quite pleased with the six suggestions I recommended our company make, which resulted in our firm producing quantifiable results for our clients at a rate of 8% faster than in previous months."

How to Impress Public Interviewers

Public interviews may appear daunting and challenging but you will have no trouble impressing your interviewers using the following tricks of the trade.

Before you begin to answer any of the interviewer's questions, take a brief moment of silence to pause and think about your answer; the amount of time you choose to be silent is up to you but you do not want to wait too long to answer and be consistent with the length of each of your pauses. This may feel a bit weird at first but if you remain silent before answering every question, both you and the interviewer will become more comfortable with the habit as the interview progress. The interviewer will not think you are dimwitted, slow, or have trouble formulating good answers under pressure; instead, the interviewer will view your habitual pause as an indication you are self-disciplined and wise for thinking before you speak.

After your brief pause, repeat the interviewer's question out loud for all attendees present to hear because in some cases the interviewer is not permitted to repeat the question. There are two benefits for interviewees when they choose to restate questions out loud before answering them:

   \1. The interviewer will think the interviewee is paying close attention and really wants the job

\E If the interviewee misunderstands the question and their answer is way off-base, the interviewer will be able to empathize because they can more easily follow the interviewee's train-of-thought/logic because the interviewee restated the question out loud before answering

Conversely, if the interviewee did not repeat the interviewer's question out loud then the interviewer may give them a low grade because the interviewer might think their answer was irrationally far off the mark.

Panel Interviews

Panel Interviews can be used at any time throughout both the private and public interview process, and they are quite challenging in their own regard.

Panel interviews can consist of three people or there can be upwards of a dozen people in attendance assessing the job applicant. Employers will sometimes choose to separate the panel interviewers to conduct one-on-one interviews with the interviewee. The interviews may take place on the phone, in person, via video chat, back-to-back on the same day, or employers may opt to spread the panel interviews out over an unspecified number of days or even weeks.

Each panelist may have a different role they are asked to play in order to increase the degree of difficulty of the interview. One panelist may play the role of a good cop to convey the notion they really like the interviewee; another panelist may play the role of a bad cop to assess how the interviewee handled the added stress; still, another panelist may play the role of a *"bad"* bad cop in hopes of making the interviewee feel really uncomfortable.

One example of this behavior for example could be that the bad cop may never smile, he or she may aggressively take notes, and ask extremely difficult questions; while, the *"bad"* bad cop might stare at the interviewee non-stop with folded arms, maintain an unpleasant or displeased look on their face, pace the room while staring at the interviewee, or even shake their head in disagreement to the interviewee's answers.

How to Impress a Panel

Despite the perceived difficulty of panel interviews, success is not out of reach and with practice you can ace every panel interview you encounter. Reread *Chapter 4: Attitude: How to Display Confidence During Your Interview* to refresh your memory.

Take turns making eye contact with each panelist, including the ones playing the role of a bad cop and a *"bad"* bad cop. Consistent eye contact combined with a gentle smile shows self-confidence, respect, and interest in the interview process.

First make direct eye contact with the interviewer who asked you the question, then repeat the question out loud, and during your answer take turns making eye contact with each of the panelists in attendance. Also, make certain that all of your answers are truthful and concise in order to give a good impression.

Throughout this process, remember the basic rules of interview etiquette regardless of how nervous you may be. Calmly clasp your hands together and place them in your lap for the duration of the interview, and be mindful of your body language including posture and the position of your legs—crossed for gentlemen, or discreetly tucked for ladies.

This all may take some time before it feels comfortable and becomes second nature to you but remember *perfect practice makes perfect*.

HELPFUL TIPS:

- ✓ Behavioral questions will give you a clue as to what quality or trait the interviewer wants you to include in your answer.
- ✓ After you answer the interviewer's question, make sure to briefly tie in your answer to the position for which you're applying.

SUMMARY NOTES:

1. Companies hire people who are concise and direct when answering questions.
2. STAR stands for Situation, Task, Action, Result.
3. Use the STAR method to organize and craft your answers.
4. Remember to quantify your experiences in each of your answers.
5. Pause briefly before every answer then repeat the interviewer's question out loud.
6. Align all answers to the position you seek.
7. Take turns making eye contact with every panelist.
8. Clasp your hands together and place them in your lap.
9. Gentlemen cross your legs at the knees.
10. Ladies, sit towards the edge of your chair, angle yourself, and cross your legs at the ankles.
11. Perfect practice makes perfect.

Chapter 7

Tips for Ex-Convicts

Ex-offenders, it's like Ben Franklin said,
the constitution only guarantees the right to pursue happiness,
you have to catch it yourself.
The power to make a positive new beginning
rests in your hands, head and heart.
Take advantage of the tremendous resources available to you and
make every effort to grab hold of the American dream.
—Kenyen Brown

Keynote:

Companies hire people who show genuine remorse for their misdeeds.

Objective:

Be upfront, make zero excuses, and display a burning desire to earn the opportunity to be given a second chance.

Difficulty in Landing a Job as an Ex-offender

It is unfortunate but all too true nonetheless, that the mistakes of someone's youth will haunt them for the rest of their life. An article published in 2011 by Prison Legal News depicted a 2008 study about ex-offenders: [iii]

- 90% of the people convicted of a felony are males
- 13.9 million working-age ex-felons—1 in 8 men was an ex-felon
- 36% of ex-prisoners had not earned a high school diploma or GED compared to 10% of general population
- Only 11% of former prisoners took any college courses compared to 60% of general population
- 40% of the prison population was African Americans compared to 15% of the U.S. population
- 20% of the prison population was Latinos compared to 15% of the U.S. population
- 30% of adult offenders released from prison are re-arrested within the first 6 months
- 67% of ex-offenders are re-arrested within 3 years of their release—that is 2 out of 3

When you are released from prison you will most likely have an **extremely difficult** time landing a job:

- 15–30% less likely to get hired if you were incarcerated
- Only 40% of employers would consider hiring job applicants with criminal histories
- Less likely to get hired for jobs involving money or customer service
- 50% of the 262,000 federal prisoners released from prison between 2002–2006 could not secure any employment during their supervised release

The good news is that **93%** of the ex-offenders **who secured employment** during the entirety of their supervised release were able to successfully reintegrate back into society and **did not return to prison.**[iv]

Resources to Help Ex-offenders Find Jobs

Do not give up hope if you were released from incarceration and you are having a difficult time landing a job. There are dozens of programs and websites that are dedicated to lending a helping hand to ex-convicts. Make sure to do your part and reach out to a few of the available programs in your area that are willing to assist you with your employment search.

One program that does this is Project H.O.P.E. —Helping Offenders Pursue Excellence—which helps ex-offenders make the transition back into main stream society by addressing their housing, educational, and employment needs.

The following websites are also excellent resources to help ex-offenders find local programs in their state to assist them in finding employment:

- www.exoffenders.net
- www.helpforfelons.org/reentry-programs-ex-offenders-state
- www.felonopportunities.com

\E www.freedomforfelonz.com

The following books provide wonderful insights to the tumultuous experience of recidivism:

\E *Jobs For Felons* by Michael Ford

\E *Support Programs for Ex-Offenders: A State-By-State Directory* by Harry Spiller

\E *The Ex-Offender's Job Hunting Guide: 10 Steps to a New Life in the Work World* by Ron Krannich and Caryl Krannich

\E *Beyond Bars: Rejoining Society After Prison* by Jeffrey Ian Ross and Stephen C. Richards

Be Upfront During Interviews

Review *Chapter 1: How to Land an Interview* to learn about additional resources that can help you secure job interviews such as soliciting a recruiter to do most of the leg work for you.

After your hard work pays off and you land some interviews, be upfront and candidly tell your interviewers that you have prior convictions, but do not sabotage yourself and state your offenses at the beginning of interviews unless the interviewer brings it up. Instead, during a pause somewhere in the interview, broach the subject with humility and admit that you had problems in the past that you did not want to appear to be hiding from the interviewer.

Be sure to ask for a second chance to display your work ethic and trustworthiness.

Briefly give an overview of your charge, look the interviewer in the eyes, and tell them that you accept full responsibility and you refuse to make any excuses for your actions.

In addition, ex-offenders **should not** do any of the following:

- Avoid discussing their convictions until their background check disqualifies them
- Lie about their convictions
- Blame others
- Attempt to change the flow of the conversation
- Give more information about their convictions than what was asked
- Avoid eye contact
- Fidget, play with hands, or make distracting hand gestures
- Get angry or respond defensively

Interviewers do not like hearing excuses; instead, they prefer for interviewees to own up to their mistakes and display sincerity when stating that they will not repeat similar offenses in the future.

Tip to Get Offered the Job

During the interview, ex-offenders should go an extra step to display to their interviewers that they are thirsty to receive a job offer. Ex-offenders can offer to work as an unpaid intern for a specified amount of time so their employer can get a glimpse of their discipline, work habits, teamwork capabilities, punctuality, along with their capacity to learn new information quickly.

A probationary period of fourteen to twenty one days should give a potential employer plenty of time to assess the interviewee, which may inch the ex-offender one step closer to securing employment. No one enjoys working for free of course, but such a temporary setback could pay-off exponentially in the long run. Sometimes the patience we must muster to make sacrifices today, leads to a wealthier and healthier tomorrow. If you want that job bad enough, I suggest telling your interviewer that you are willing to work as an unpaid intern for a specified amount of time in hopes of garnering a paid position upon the completion of your probationary period.

I am extremely proud of each of you for doing your part to make the necessary changes in your life in order to pursue the goals you have for tomorrow! Change is rarely easy. However, I believe if you write down your goals, seek help, do not make excuses, strengthen your strengths, and persevere, that you will one day accomplish your goals, whatever they may be.

HELPFUL TIPS:

- ✓ There are companies that make it a priority to hire ex-offenders such as Gallery Furniture.
- ✓ Read my book *The Purpose of College Simplified: Options after High School, Obtaining Success & Choosing a Career* to learn if you need college to be successful.
- ✓ Do not repeat your mistakes from yesterday.
- ✓ There are people willing to help you if you make an effort.

SUMMARY NOTES:

1. Do not choose a life of crime.
2. Ex-offenders have an extremely difficult time finding employment after their release.
3. Ex-offenders who secure employment during the entirety of their supervised release are less likely to return to prison.
4. Dozens of resources are available to help ex-offenders reacclimatize to society.
5. Do not sabotage yourself and state your offenses at the beginning of interviews unless the interviewer brings it up.
6. Inform your interviewer about your convictions during a pause somewhere in the interview, broach the subject with humility, admit that you had problems in the past, and ask for a second chance to display your work ethic and trustworthiness.
7. Implement excellent non-verbal communication during your interview.

8. Offer to work as an unpaid intern for a probationary period of 14–21 days to earn your employers trust.

9. Change is rarely easy.

10. You will one day accomplish your goals if you write down your goals, seek help, do not make excuses, strengthen your strengths, and persevere.

11. I am very proud of each and every one of you!

Judge a man by his questions rather than by his answers.
—Voltaire

Keynote:

Companies hire people who ask insightful, open-ended questions.

Objective:

Ask astute questions that are pertinent to the position for which you are applying.

Ask Intelligent Questions to Woo Your Interviewers

Before you delve into this chapter, first reread *Chapter 5: How to Ace a Private Interview* and *Chapter 6: How to Ace a Public Interview* because they contain cornerstone techniques that you will first need to master.

To make your questions more challenging, ask your interviewer to give a minimum of three examples. In my experience, asking for less than three examples is too easy but asking for six or more examples tends to be too difficult, and you run the risk of annoying them.

Feel free to ask for three to five examples during your line of questioning.

An example of asking for 3–5 examples:

Darren Olson, Candidate:

"What are *three* aspects of your management or leadership style that you would like to improve?"

Jeanelle Gardiner, Interviewer:

"Excellent question, Darren. I want to improve my task delegation, nonverbal communication, and my organizational skills."

Interview Structure

Typically, no two interviews are exactly the same. Your interview may be conducted face-to-face or via the telephone; at the company office or a restaurant; in the morning or the afternoon. You may be interviewed by one person or a panel; the interviewer's questions may be in-depth or succinct; or you may encounter any combination of the aforementioned ten possibilities. Although your interview experience may vary, there is a relatively recognizable format to which most interviewers adhere.

Usually, the first portion of most interviews focuses on ice-breaker questions. Ice-breaker questions appear at the beginning of conversations and are designed to ease tension or relieve formality while introducing each party.

This phase of an interview gives the interviewee an excellent opportunity to ask the interviewer about their personal life, prior occupations, favorite cities, birthplace, favorite sports teams, etc., in order to get the interviewer to talk more than the interviewee. After you answer your interviewer's ice-breaker inquiry, do your best to respond with a similar question and be sure to include *follow-up* questions whenever appropriate.

An example of ice-breaker follow-up questions:

Clint Avants, Interviewer:

"Have you lived here all your life?"

Michelle Murphy, Candidate:

"Actually, I was born in Houston, Texas but we moved to Crested Butte, Colorado when I was seven years old. What about yourself; are you from this area or have you relocated from somewhere else?"

Clint Avants, Interviewer:

"I was born in San Antonio, Texas and lived there till I moved away for college in Austin, Texas."

Michelle Murphy, Candidate:

"What college in Austin? And what was your major?"

A second example of ice-breaker follow-up questions:

Bryan Hynson, Interviewer:

"So, tell me a little about yourself."

Michael Quach, Candidate:

"I enjoy computer programming and traveling is another passion of mine. For instance, just last month my wife—Polica—and I vacationed on the island of Grenada, and I must say it was a phenomenal experience. We both really enjoyed our stay on that mountainous tropical beauty. If I may ask, have you ever visited the Caribbean, and if so, what parts?"

Bryan Hynson, Interviewer:

"I went to Puerto Rico a couple years ago for a wedding, and I went to Jamaica just last year."

Michael Quach, Candidate:

"Oh, I think Puerto Rico's beaches are absolutely breathtaking. So, what activities did you do while you were visiting Puerto Rico and Jamaica?"

The second portion of an interview generally focuses on the interviewee's educational background and employment history. Answer all of your interviewer's questions honestly but gauge the amount of time you use for responding, because *less* is *more*. This facet of an interview gives the interviewee meager opportunities to ask *open-ended, follow-up* questions, but if an opportunity presents itself, be sure to take full advantage.

An example of an employment history follow-up question:

Jeremy Rachel, Interviewer:

"What were some of your responsibilities at Cowboy Transportation & Logistics?"

Harun Griffiths, Candidate:

"I developed financial models, including forecasting, margin analysis, and pricing in order to coordinate efforts between the sales team, truck drivers, and the marketing team. Also, I oversaw the design and printing of all marketing paraphernalia. What departments did you work in when you first started in the trucking business?"

Jeremy Rachel, Interviewer:

"That was such a long time ago, might I remind you, before cell phones and pagers even existed. I started working part-time at a truck stop, cleaning bathrooms twice a week or doing whatever handyman work that was needed. After graduating from school I took a job working the 23-channel CB radio for a ten-person company. The boss liked my work ethic, so he started giving me more responsibilities, which eventually brought me to this position."

The third and final portion of an interview is the interviewee's million-dollar opportunity. Customarily, the interviewer asks the interviewee if they have any questions. This is the perfect chance for the interviewee to ask some of the 60 questions I propose in this chapter. In addition, ask plenty of *open-ended, follow-up* questions but continually gauge both the interviewer's nonverbal and verbal cues to determine how many questions you should ask. If your interviewer is receptive, continue your inquiries until they show signs of annoyance, the allotted time has expired, or you have gathered all of the information you seek.

Photocopy or write down my list of 60 questions to take with you to the interview.

60 Thought-Provoking Questions to Ask Your

Interviewer

Question # 1:

What is your company's three-month plan, six-month plan, one-year plan, and five-year plan?

In the third and final portion of the interview, when your interviewer asks if you have any questions, ask this question first. It will catch your interviewer off guard, it will set the tone for the remainder of the interview, and it will thoroughly engage your interviewer right from the jump.

This question will instantly make your interviewer think you are taking this interview process very seriously, you came equipped with insightful questions, and you want to know what makes the company tick. Equally important, this question will give your interviewer the impression that you are very interested in the company's short-term and long-term goals, that you are goal-oriented, organized, and interested in working for the company for the long haul. Also, your interviewer will observe that you are intuitive, analytical, and intelligent. The remaining fifty-nine questions can be asked in the order of your choosing.

Question # 2:

Will this company remain privately held or do the decision-makers plan to take this company public? If the latter, within what timeframe do you believe the decision-makers will take the company public?

Do not ask this question if the company you are interviewing with is a publicly traded company. The following are a few suggestions to determine if a company is public or private before your interview begins:

A) If the company's stock is sold on an exchange, then it is a publicly traded company. Quite a few publicly traded companies provide information on their website about their stock. Search the company's website for a link titled "investor relations" or a similar heading.

B) Use this website <https://www.sec.gov/edgar/searchedgar/companysearch.html> to find reports on publicly traded companies. It is a free web database provided by the U.S. Securities and Exchange Commission (SEC). Go to the website and enter the company name.

C) Call the company and ask the administrative assistant if the company is private or public.

Question # 3:

What are four things you love about this company?

Question # 4:

What are four things you would change about this company?

Question # 5:

What are four things you would change at this particular office?

Question # 6:

What were four factors that contributed to your advancement within the company?

Question # 7:

What characteristics do you think best define a leader, and why?

Sit patiently and wait for a response. If your interviewer struggles to answer, offer clarification by saying, "Do you think it is more important for a leader to be a certain age? Do you perceive charisma to be more important or attention to detail, for example?"

Question # 8:

Which leadership styles do you most closely exemplify?

Wait quietly for an answer. The following are ten leadership styles, in case your interviewer needs clarification:

A) Transactional Leadership

This leadership style starts with the idea that team members agree to obey their leader when they accept a job. The "transaction" usually involves the organization paying team members in return for their effort and compliance. The leader has a right to "punish" team members if their work does not meet an appropriate standard.

Although this might sound controlling and paternalistic, transactional leadership offers some benefits. For one, this leadership style clarifies everyone's roles and responsibilities. Another benefit is that, because transactional leadership judges team members on performance, people who are ambitious or who are motivated by external rewards—including compensation— often thrive.

The downside of this leadership style is that team members can do little to improve their job satisfaction. It can feel stifling and it can lead to high staff turnover.

Transactional leadership is really a type of management, not a true leadership style, because the focus is on short-term tasks. It has serious limitations for knowledge-based or creative work. It can, however, be effective in other situations.

B) Autocratic Leadership

Autocratic leadership is an extreme form of transactional leadership, where leaders have complete power over their people. Staff and team members have little opportunity to make suggestions, even if these would be in the team's or the organization's best interest.

The benefit of autocratic leadership is that it is incredibly efficient. Decisions are made quickly; work gets done.

The downside, conversely, is that most people resent being treated this way. Therefore, autocratic leadership often leads to high levels of absenteeism and high staff turnover. However, the style can be effective for some routine and unskilled jobs; in these situations, the advantages of control may outweigh the disadvantages.

Autocratic leadership is often best used in crises, when decisions must be made quickly and without dissent. For instance, the military often uses an autocratic leadership style; top commanders are responsible for quickly making complex decisions, which allows troops to focus their attention and energy on performing their allotted tasks and missions.

C) Bureaucratic Leadership

Bureaucratic leaders work "by the book." They follow rules rigorously and ensure that their people follow procedures precisely.

This is an appropriate leadership style for work involving serious safety risks (such as working with machinery, with toxic substances, or at dangerous heights) or where large sums of money are involved. Bureaucratic leadership is also useful in organizations where employees do routine tasks—as in manufacturing.

The downside of this leadership style is that it is ineffective in teams and organizations that rely on flexibility, creativity, or innovation.

Much of the time, bureaucratic leaders achieve their position because of their ability to conform to and uphold rules, not because of their qualifications or expertise. This can cause resentment when team members feel as though their expertise or advice is not appreciated.

D) Transformational Leadership

Transformational leadership is often the best leadership style to use in business situations.

Transformational leaders are inspiring because they expect the best from everyone on their team as well as themselves. This leads to high productivity and engagement from everyone on their team.

The downside of transformational leadership is that while the leader's enthusiasm is passed onto the team, he or she can need to be supported by "detail people."

That is why, in many organizations, both transactional and transformational leadership styles are useful. Transactional leaders—or managers—ensure that routine work is done reliably, while transformational leaders look after initiatives that add new value. It is also important to use other leadership styles when necessary—this will depend on the people you are leading and the situation that you are in.

E) Charismatic Leadership

A charismatic leadership style can resemble transformational leadership because these leaders inspire enthusiasm in their teams and are energetic in motivating others to move forward. This excitement and commitment from teams is an enormous benefit.

The difference between charismatic leaders and transformational leaders lies in their intention. Transformational leaders want to transform their teams and organizations. Charismatic leaders are often focused on themselves and may not want to change anything.

The downside to charismatic leaders is that they can believe more in themselves than in their teams. This can create the risk that a project or even an entire organization might collapse if the leader leaves. A charismatic leader might believe that he or she can do no wrong, even when others are warning them about the path they are on; this feeling of invincibility can ruin a team or an organization.

Also, in the followers' eyes, success is directly connected to the presence of the charismatic leader. As such, charismatic leadership carries great responsibility and it needs a long-term commitment from the leader.

F) Democratic / Participative Leadership

Democratic leaders make the final decisions but they include team members in the decision-making process. They encourage creativity and team members are often highly engaged in projects and decisions.

There are many benefits of democratic leadership. Team members tend to have high job satisfaction and are productive because they are more involved in decisions. This style also helps develop people's skills. Team members feel in control of their destiny, so they are motivated to work hard by more than just a financial reward.

Because participation takes time, this approach can slow decision-making but the result is often good. The approach can be most suitable when working as a team is essential and when quality is more important than efficiency or productivity.

The downside of democratic leadership is that it can often hinder situations where speed or efficiency is essential. For instance, during a crisis, a team can waste valuable time gathering people's input. Another downside is that some team members might not have the knowledge or expertise to provide high-quality input.

G) Laissez-Faire Leadership

This French phrase means "leave it be" and it describes leaders who allow their people to work on their own. This type of leadership can also occur naturally, when managers do not have sufficient control over their work and their people.

Laissez-faire leaders may give their team complete freedom to do their work and set their own deadlines. They provide team support with resources and advice, if needed, but otherwise do not get involved.

This leadership style can be effective if the leader monitors performance and gives feedback to team members regularly. It is most likely to be effective when individual team members are experienced, skilled self-starters.

The main benefit of laissez-faire leadership is that giving team members so much autonomy can lead to high job satisfaction and increased productivity.

The downside is that it can be damaging if team members do not manage their time well or if they do not have the knowledge, skills, or motivation to do their work effectively.

H) Task-Oriented Leadership

Task-oriented leaders focus only on getting the job done and can be autocratic. They actively define the work and the roles required, put structures in place, and plan, organize, and monitor work. These leaders also perform other key tasks, such as creating and maintaining standards for performance. The benefit of task-oriented leadership is that it ensures that deadlines are met and it is especially useful for team members who do not manage their time well.

However, because task-oriented leaders do not tend to think much about their team's well-being, this approach can share many of the flaws of autocratic leadership, including causing motivation and retention problems.

I) People-Oriented / Relations-Oriented Leadership

With people-oriented leadership, leaders are totally focused on organizing, supporting, and developing the people on their teams. This is a participatory style and tends to encourage good teamwork and creative collaboration. This is the opposite of task-oriented leadership.

People-oriented leaders treat everyone on the team equally. They are friendly and approachable, they pay attention to the welfare of everyone in the group, and they make themselves available whenever team members need help or advice.

The benefit of this leadership style is that people-oriented leaders create teams that everyone wants to be part of. Team members are often more productive and willing to take risks, because they know that the leader will provide support if they need it.

The downside is that some leaders can take this approach too far; they may put the development of their team above tasks or project directives.

J) Servant Leadership

This term, created by Robert Greenleaf in the 1970s, describes a leader often not formally recognized as such. When someone at any level within an organization leads simply by meeting the needs of the team, he or she can be described as a "servant leader."

Servant leaders often lead by example. They have high integrity and lead with generosity.

In many ways, servant leadership is a form of democratic leadership because the whole team tends to be involved in decision making. However, servant leaders often "lead from behind," preferring to stay out of the limelight and letting their team accept recognition for their hard work.

Supporters of the servant leadership model suggest that it is a good way to move ahead in a world where values are increasingly important and where servant leaders can achieve power because of their values, ideals, and ethics. This is an approach that can help to create a positive corporate culture and can lead to high morale among team members.

However, other people believe that in competitive leadership situations, people who practice servant leadership can find themselves left behind by leaders using other leadership styles. This leadership style also takes time to apply correctly; it is ill-suited to situations where you have to make quick decisions or meet tight deadlines.

Although you can use servant leadership in many situations, it is often most practical in politics, or in positions where leaders are elected to serve a team, committee, organization, or community.[v]

Question # 9:

Can you please describe which leadership style most closely exemplifies the immediate supervisor for this position?

If your interviewer will also be your immediate supervisor then ask question # 8 instead.

Question # 10:

What are four values that best exemplify this company?

Question # 11:

What are three qualities you most admire in your best employee?

Question # 12:

What were three qualities you disliked in the last employee that you let go?

If your interviewer is stumped, ask them, "What were three qualities you have disliked in anyone who you have seen get fired from this company during your tenure?"

Question # 13:

Do you find it easier to fire someone or hire someone, and why?

There is no inherent right or wrong answer; instead, your interviewer's answer will reveal their thought process and logic. I, personally, believe it is much easier to fire someone because over a period of time you will have factual evidence as to a person's work ethic, character, and value system. When you hire someone, in contrast, you are assuming that person will be a good fit for the firm, with very little data to substantiate your hypothesis.

Question # 14:

Why did my predecessor leave this job?

Possible *follow-up* question: "Is the company looking for one replacement or is the company hiring multiple people for this position?"

Question # 15:

What are the next four steps in this interview process?

Question # 16:

How would you best describe your management style?

Sit quietly and wait for a response. If your interviewer asks for clarification, then clarify by saying, "For example, do you find micromanagement to be more effective than another style of management?"

Question # 17:

What were the last three books you read, and do you have any good suggestions that I might look up?

Question # 18:

What is your preferred method of communicating with your team, and why?

Question # 19:

What metrics will be used to measure my success within the first six months of accepting this position, and why?

Question # 20:

Are the same metrics used to evaluate employees in superior positions, including the immediate supervisor to *this* position? Why?

Question # 21:

Would you prefer to earn less money but receive more benefits, or would you prefer to make more money but receive fewer benefits? Why do you feel this way?

This is a great in-depth question to decipher the priorities of your interviewer. Most people assume the word *benefits* refer solely to medical or healthcare. However, in this instance the term *benefits* actually refer to time off, vacation days, sick days, healthcare, work remotely, bonuses, etc. Ideally, your interviewer will inquire about your definition of *benefits* before they answer because they will want to gather as much information as possible before making a decision. There is no inherent right or wrong answer; instead, your interviewer's answer will let you know if they most value money, family time, or security over risk, for instance.

Question # 22:

Can you please explain the compensation and benefit packages available with this position?

You are welcome to briefly touch on the topic of salary and benefits during your first interview; however, do not focus a large amount of time on discussing compensation. You are liable to eliminate yourself prematurely if you focus too many of your questions on compensation. You should, instead, spend the majority of your time inquiring about the duties of the position, the expectations of your employer, and the management style of your supervisors throughout the first interview. The compensation and benefit packages will be discussed more in depth when you make it to the second and third rounds of the interview process.

Question # 23:

In what capacity does your company encourage higher education?

Wait patiently for a response. If your interviewer asks for clarification, then say, "Does the company have a reimbursement or incentive package for those who wish to gain further education?"

Question # 24:

What are three things about my candidacy that might keep you from offering me the position, and why?

Question # 25:

What was the employee turnover rate over the past eighteen months?

Question # 26:

Thinking back to people who have been in this position previously, what were four things that differentiated employees who were good from employees who were really great?

Question # 27:

What are five work-related challenges that I may face within the first three months of accepting this position?

Question # 28:

If I come up with a new idea that had never been implemented at this company, what are your processes, along with compensation allotment, to bring that idea to fruition?

Question # 29:

What are five short-term corporate goals that you have devised for yourself?

Question # 30:

What are five long-term corporate goals that you have devised for yourself?

Question # 31:

What are four strengths of my immediate supervisor?

Question # 32:

What are four weaknesses of my immediate supervisor?

Question # 33:

What are three things you would change about your boss or supervisors?

Question # 34:

What has been your legacy thus far with this company?

Question # 35:

What do you want your legacy at this company to be after you leave?

Question # 36:

How many people have you mentored at this company?

Question # 37:

Can you please name three people at this firm who have had a positive influence on you, and why?

Question # 38:

What are four ways you have impacted this company for the better?

Question # 39:

What are five resources that will be readily available to help me perform my job with the utmost efficiency?

Question # 40:

What are three things about me that have impressed you thus far, and why?

Question # 41:

What motivates or drives you to succeed, and why?

Question # 42:

What are three ways this company supports a work/life balance?

Question # 43:

What are three things your personal friends outside of the company like about this company, and why?

Question # 44:

Please describe a prior situation when management did not live up to the company's values. How was the matter resolved?

Question # 45:

What circumstances brought you to this company?

Question # 46:

What are three of your corporate regrets at this company, and why?

Question # 47:

By what date do you expect to make a hiring decision?

Question # 48:

Can you please recommend three people within this department who would be excellent mentors for me, and why?

Be sure to write down the three names that your interviewer recommends. This question forces your interviewer to begin to picture you working for the company. Remember, success must first be visualized before it can be achieved. If your interviewer has difficulty finding three people who fit the mentor role, a red flag should be raised about the quality of the firm's current employees.

Question # 49:

Can you describe a time where you disagreed with your supervisors please? How was the matter resolved?

Question # 50:

Can you give me an example of a time you went above and beyond for one of your employees please?

Question # 51:

When do you feel the most satisfied at your current position?

Question # 52:

Can you tell me about a time you had to give an employee negative feedback? How did you and the employee handle it?

Question # 53:

What is the most difficult decision you made in the last three years and how did you come to that decision?

Question # 54:

How long did it take for you to make a contribution or establish your legacy at this firm?

Question # 55:

How many of your suggestions for improvement were approved and implemented by your superiors? Please describe at least one of them.

Question # 56:

Can you name three people in your whole career who really made a difference in your life please?

Question # 57:

Who are three of your mentors at this company and how have they helped you accomplish your goals to date?

Question # 58:

When disagreements arise between you and an employee, how would you prefer the employee address the matter?

Question # 59:

Which executive or manager at this firm do you respect the most, and why?

Question # 60:

When do I start?

Ask this question last coupled with a gentle smile and a humble tone. Your goal should be to impress your interviewers with your nonverbal and verbal communication throughout the interview process in order to receive an employment offer. This is an excellent question to respectively, yet succinctly sum up your goal and it may prompt your interviewer to offer you a position on the spot.

HELPFUL TIPS:

- ✓ In group interviews, take turns making eye contact with each panelist when you are answering a question.

- ✓ Make sure to ask follow-up questions to each of my 60 questions before you proceed to ask another question from the list.

- ✓ The art and science of asking questions is the source of all knowledge. —Thomas Berger

SUMMARY NOTES:

1. Ask insightful, open-ended questions to impress your interviewer.

2. DO NOT answer questions with excessive amounts of detail.

3. Ask *open-ended, follow-up questions* whenever appropriate.

4. Respond nonverbally with head nods and gentle smiles while your interviewer is speaking.

5. Answer all of your interviewer's questions honestly.

6. Gauge the interviewer's nonverbal and verbal cues to determine if you should continue to ask questions.

7. If your interviewer does not respond immediately to your questions, sit quietly and wait for his/her response without offering clarification. Clarify your inquiries only at your interviewer's request.

Good manners will open doors that the best education cannot.
—Clarence Thomas

Keynote:

Companies hire people who are respectful in person, on the phone, and in emails.

Objective:

Manifest respect in your speech and in your actions.

Show a Great Deal of Respect to Everyone

It is imperative you display respect to your interviewer and to whomever you come into contact with at the interviewing company. The easiest way to exhibit respect is to say Mr. / Ms., and the person's last name every time you address them. Resist the urge to call them by their first name unless that person insists you do so.

An example of verbal respect:

Job Candidate:

"Good morning. I have an eleven a.m. interview with Ms. Dinges. I'm sorry, what is your name?"

Administrative Assistant:

"Good morning to you as well. My name is Vaughn Henry. And what is your name?"

Job Candidate:

"My name is Lauren Murry. Thanks for asking."

Administrative Assistant:

"Nice to meet you, Ms. Murry. Have a seat and Ms. Dinges will be with you shortly. Would you like some coffee or water while you wait?"

Job Candidate:

"No thank you, Mr. Henry. But thank you kindly for the offer."

A second example of verbal respect:

Interviewer:

"Hello, Lauren. I hope I did not keep you waiting too long. I apologize for the messiness in advance, but please come in."

Candidate:

"Good morning, Ms. Dinges. It is a pleasure to finally meet you face to face. And the wait was not long at all."

Interviewer:

"Oh, please, call me Lindsey. Ms. Dinges makes me feel old."

Candidate:

"Sounds good, Lindsey."

Post-Interview Follow-up

Drop off a handwritten thank-you card within twenty-four hours to the secretary of the department in which you interviewed. Thank-you cards are highly effective. The act conveys respect, it gives both the secretary and your interviewer yet another positive perception of you, and most importantly, it forces your interviewer to recall information about you from the prior day's interview. In that moment of recollection, your interviewer will seek to remember the outfit you wore, thought-provoking questions you asked, and your projected attitude throughout the interview. The personalized thank-you card intelligently yet unobtrusively burns a lasting image of you in your interviewer's mind.

It is also perfectly acceptable to periodically contact your recruiter or interviewer to find out if you got the job. However, there are a few guidelines to follow in order to avoid crossing the line into intrusion.

First, do not contact your recruiter or your interviewer more than once in any given week unless you receive permission to do otherwise. I recommend you follow up every two weeks so as not to become a nuisance. Another way to display persistence without appearing overbearing is to ask your interviewer's consent to contact them at a specific date and time in the future. Your interviewer will then suggest a different date or time if your suggestion does not fit their schedule. Keep in mind that consistent follow-up, when executed correctly, can be viewed as a positive attribute more readily recognized as persistence. Second, find out which communication method—email or telephone—is preferred by your interviewer, then proceed accordingly. Third, be patient and remain positive, because depending on the position you are seeking, it may take a couple of months to get a conclusive answer. Finally, while you wait patiently, continue to seek out interviews with other companies for positions you desire.

Email Etiquette

Two-thirds of interviewees take email etiquette for granted but your emails can be the difference maker that prompts your interviewer to hire you. First, begin every email with Mr. / Ms. and the person's last name. Next, incorporate a few of the following greetings into your emails but be sure to use a different greeting each time:

> ✓ I hope this email finds you well

- I hope you had a blessed weekend
- I hope you are having a blessed week thus far
- I hope you are having a blessed day
- I hope your day is going well thus far
- Good morning
- Good afternoon
- Good evening
- I hope today finds you in good spirits
- I hope you had a restful weekend
- I hope you are having a pleasant morning
- I hope you are having a pleasant afternoon
- I hope you are having a pleasant evening
- I hope you are having a pleasant week thus far
- Thank you for the opportunity to interview with your firm
- Thank you once again for this opportunity
- Thank you for taking the time to speak with me
- Thank you for taking the time to meet with me

Also, close every email with one of the following closings but be sure to never use the same closing consecutively:

- With great appreciation
- Thanks in advance
- Thank you
- Thank you for this opportunity
- Kind regards
- Sincerely

- Most sincerely
- Best wishes
- Best regards
- Wishing you well
- Many thanks
- Kind wishes
- With sincere thanks
- Warm regards
- Warm wishes
- Thank you for your consideration
- God bless
- Gratefully yours
- Most gratefully
- Very gratefully
- Most obliged
- Thank you once again
- Thank you once again for this opportunity

An example of a respectful follow-up email:

Mr. Frame,

I hope you had a restful weekend. I am touching base to get an update on my application status, and to find out if more information is needed from me at this time.

Thank you for this opportunity, and I look forward to hearing from you.

Best wishes,
Jenny Ann

A second example of a respectful follow-up email:

Good afternoon, Kendal Mathews,

Thank you once again for the opportunity to interview with your firm and I hope this email finds you well. Per your request, I completed the Disclosure Release form and attached it to this email. If you are unable to view the attachment please let me know and I will be more than happy to rescan it and fax it to you tomorrow. Second, pertaining to dates, please note that I am available to be sent to Scottsdale, Arizona as soon as possible, and I have no scheduling conflicts at this time. I also plan to submit my required/requested drug test tomorrow.

Do not hesitate to contact me if any questions or concerns involving my situation should arise. Thank you once again, and I look forward to moving forward with the interview process.

With great appreciation,
Brandon Paul Hamm

After you have written your email, run a spell check and read it over slowly at least twice before you press *send*. The best times to send emails are between 8:00 a.m. and 10:00 a.m. or between 3:00 p.m. and 4:00 p.m. The optimal days to send emails are Tuesdays, Wednesdays, or Thursdays, because most interviewers are out of the office on Saturday and Sunday. On Monday, they may be in meetings and unavailable to deal with outside questions or issues. On Friday, most interviewers are interested in wrapping things up in preparation for the weekend, or finishing work for important deadlines and thus are unavailable for follow-ups and outside concerns. Also, avoid sending emails around holidays or any major vacation times. Do your best to pick a day and time when your interviewer will be the most likely to respond but do not stress about the launch time.[vi]

HELPFUL TIPS:

✓ Open doors for both men and women who are walking either in front of or behind you.

✓ Say *"yes sir,"* and *"yes ma'am,"* or *"no sir"* and *"no ma'am,"* instead of simply saying *"yes"* or *"no"*.

✓ Make sure to spell and pronounce your interviewer's name correctly EVERY TIME!

✓ Do not use any abbreviations in your emails; instead, be sure to spell out each and every word.

✓ Every one of us is an artist, and as an artist, you really can stroll into any venue that you want, as long as you take your time to learn the etiquette of that venue. —Terrence Howard

SUMMARY NOTES:

1. Companies hire people who are respectful in person, on the phone, and in emails.

2. Show a great deal of respect to anyone who works at the company at which you are interviewing.

3. Say Mr. / Ms. and the person's last name every time you address them, unless that person insists you call them by their first name.

4. Drop off a personalized thank-you card within 24 hours to the secretary of the department in which you interviewed.

5. Do not use any abbreviations in your emails; instead, spell out every word.

6. Use a different greeting each time.

7. Never use the same closing consecutively.

8. Spell check and read over your email at least twice before you press *send.*

9. Perseverance will pay.

If you don't think your anxiety, depression, sadness and stress
impact your physical health, think again.
All of these emotions trigger chemical reactions in your body,
which can lead to inflammation and a weakened immune system.
Learn to cope, sweet friend.
There will always be dark days.
—Kris Carr

Keynote:

An estimated 350 million people of all ages suffer from
depression.

Objective:

If you have symptoms of depression, ask for help immediately.

What is Depression?

The job search process can be frustrating, disappointing,
unnerving, exiting, stressful, and at times depressing. Depression
is a medical illness with both mental and physical symptoms.
Sadness is only a small part of depression. Some people with
depression may not feel sadness at all but exhibit signs of
irritability or loss of interest in things they usually like to do.

Depression interferes with your daily life and can make it difficult to study, cause you to withdraw from school or friends, and increase your homesickness. Do not ignore or try to hide the symptoms.

It is not a character flaw that you can will it away.

There are different types of depression. The most common depressive disorders include major depression (a discrete episode, clearly different from a person's usual feeling and functioning), persistent depressive disorder (a chronic, low-grade depression that can get better or worse over time), and psychotic depression (the most severe, with delusions or hallucinations).

Some people are vulnerable to depression in the winter (seasonal affective disorder) and some women report depression in the week or two prior to their menstrual period (premenstrual dysphoric disorder). More women are affected by depression than men.

Depression Signs and Symptoms

Depression can get in the way of your ability to function with your job search and your social life. If you have been experiencing any of the following symptoms of depression nearly every day for at least 2 weeks, ask for help because you may have major depression (sometimes called "clinical depression"):[vii]

- Persistent sad, anxious, or "empty" mood
- Feelings of hopelessness, pessimism
- Feelings of guilt, worthlessness, helplessness
- Loss of interest or pleasure in hobbies and activities
- Decreased energy, fatigue, being "slowed down"
- Difficulty concentrating, remembering, or making decisions
- Difficulty sleeping, early-morning awakening, or oversleeping
- Appetite and/or unwanted weight changes
- Thoughts of death or suicide; suicide attempts
- Restlessness, irritability
- Persistent physical symptoms, such as muscle pain or headaches

Not everyone who is depressed experiences every symptom. Some people experience only a few symptoms. Some people have many symptoms. If any of these symptoms are interfering with your ability to function—or if you are having thoughts that life is not worth living or ideas of harming yourself—you should **seek help immediately**; it is not necessary to wait two weeks.

If you have thoughts of wishing you were dead or of suicide, call a helpline, such as 1-800-273-TALK (8255) for free 24-hour help, call campus security or 911, or go to the nearest emergency room.

How to Get Help for Depression

Depression can get better with care and treatment. Do not wait for depression to go away by itself or think you can manage it all on your own, and do not ignore how you are feeling just because you think you can *explain* it. As an adult, you are busy, but you need to make time to get help.

If you do not ask for help, your depression may get worse and contribute to other health problems. It can also lead to *self-medication* with high-risk behaviors that carry their own serious consequences, such as binge drinking, substance abuse, and unsafe sex.

Most cities provide mental health services through counseling centers, student health centers, or both. If you think you might have depression, start by making an appointment with a doctor or health care provider for a checkup.

Your doctor can make sure that you do not have another health problem that is causing your depression. If your doctor finds that you do not have another health problem, he or she can discuss treatment options or refer you to a mental health professional, such as a psychiatrist, counselor, or psychologist. A mental health professional can give you a thorough evaluation and also treat your depression.

How Depression Gets Treated

Effective treatments for depression include talk therapy, also called psychotherapy, medication, or a combination of talk therapy and medication. Early treatment is best.

In talk therapy, a therapist, such as a psychiatrist, a psychologist, a social worker, or counselor, can help you understand and manage your moods and feelings. You can express your emotions to someone who understands and supports you. You can also learn how to stop thinking negatively and start to look at the positives in life.

Working with your therapist will help you build confidence and feel better about yourself as you work together to find solutions to problems that may have seemed insurmountable in the depression. Research has shown that certain types of talk therapy or psychotherapy, such as those listed below, can help adults deal with depression:

- **Cognitive behavioral therapy**, or CBT, which focuses on thoughts, behaviors, and feelings related to depression
- **Interpersonal psychotherapy**, or IPT, which focuses on working on relationships
- **Dialectical behavior therapy**, or DBT, which is especially useful when depression is accompanied by self-destructive or self-harming behavior

All therapies can be adapted to each person. For example, some depression can be associated with an anxiety, social, or eating disorder. Your counseling center may offer both individual and group counseling and may also offer workshops and outreach programs to support you.

If your doctor believes that you need medication to help your depression he or she may prescribe an antidepressant. There are a number of antidepressants that have been widely studied and proven to help. If your doctor recommends medication, it is important to see your doctor regularly and tell him or her about any side effects and how you are feeling, especially if you start feeling worse or have thoughts of hurting yourself.

Although the doctor will attempt to *match* the best medication for your depression, sometimes it takes a little *trial and error* to find the best choice. If you or a close family member has done well on a particular medication in the past, that can be a good predictor of success again.

Visit the following website for further information about depression

http://www.nimh.nih.gov/health/publications/depression-and-college-students-new/index.shtml.

Additional Steps to Take

In addition to consulting a doctor and a counselor of your choice, you can also help your depression by being patient with both yourself and the process. Do not expect to get better immediately. You will experience improvement over time. Here are a few practical ways to work through depression:

- Daily exercise, spending time outside in nature and in the sun, and eating healthy foods can also help you feel better
- Get enough sleep. Try to have consistent sleep habits and avoid all-night study sessions
- Your counselor may teach you how to be aware of your feelings and some relaxation techniques. Use these when you start feeling down or upset
- Avoid using drugs and at least minimize, if not totally avoid, alcohol usage
- Break up large tasks into small ones and do what you can as you can; try not to do too many things at once
- Try to spend time with supportive family members and/or friends, and take advantage of campus resources, such as student support groups. Talk with your supportive parents, friends, and family regularly

☑ Do your best to spend time with friends and try fun things that help you express yourself. You may find that even if you do not feel like going out with friends, if you push yourself to do so, you will be able to enjoy yourself more than you thought

Remember that, by treating your depression, you are helping yourself succeed in your job search and in life.

HELPFUL TIPS:

- ✓ If you are experiencing depression, contact all of your teachers and employers to inform them of your situation so that your grades and employment will not suffer as a result.
- ✓ You are not alone in experiencing depression.
- ✓ Seek help from counselors, physicians, or outside resources to treat and manage your issues.

SUMMARY NOTES:

1. If you have symptoms of depression, ask for help.
2. Depression can get better with care and treatment.
3. Do not wait for depression to go away by itself or think you can manage it all on your own.
4. If you do not ask for help, depression may get worse and contribute to other health problems.
5. Effective treatments for depression include talk therapy (also called psychotherapy) or a combination of talk therapy and medication; early treatment is best.
6. Exercise daily, get plenty of sleep, talk to a counselor, avoid drugs, minimize alcohol usage, break up large tasks into small ones, and try to spend time with supportive family members and/or friends.
7. Perseverance will pay.
8. I am very proud of each and every one of you!

Closing Thoughts

It is my sincere hope that readers of this book were able to find at least one piece of valuable information that they can apply to their personal journey as they pursue the job of their dreams. Thank you kindly for reading my book and best of luck in your employment pursuits.

I would love to hear your feedback and perspectives so do not hesitate to reach out to me through email or social media.

Keeon@VonElijah.com
Twitter.com/VonElijahllc
Facebook.com/VonElijahllc
Instagram.com/VonElijah

[i] Mark McCormick, *Harvard Business School Goal Story*, http://www.lifemastering.com/en/harvard_school.html

[ii] Corporate Dynamix, *The Benefits of Using a Recruiter*, http://www.cdynamix.com/top-10-benefits-of-using-a-recruiter/

[iii] Prison Legal News, *Study Shows Ex-offenders Have Greatly Reduced Employment Rates* (2011), https://www.prisonlegalnews.org/news/2011/dec/15/study-shows-ex-offenders-have-greatly-reduced-employment-rates/

[iv] United States Department of Justice, *Project H.O.P.E. Re-Entry Initiative*, www.justice.gov/usao-sdal/programs/ex-offender-re-entry-initiative

[v] Mind Tools, *Leadership Styles: Choosing the Right Approach for the Situation*, http://www.mindtools.com/pages/article/newLDR_84.htm

[vi] Megan Marrs, *Perfect Timing: The Very Best Time to Send Email Newsletters* (2014), http://www.wordstream.com/blog/ws/2014/09/04/best-time-to-send-email-campaign

[vii] *Depression and College Students*, http://www.nimh.nih.gov/health/publications/depression-and-college-students-new/index.shtml

www.ingramcontent.com/pod-product-compliance
Lightning Source LLC
Chambersburg PA
CBHW071817200526
45169CB00018B/365